Technology and Society

Other Books of Related Interest:

Opposing Viewpoints Series

Biomedical Ethics

Cloning

Reproductive Technologies

Stem Cells

The Internet

Current Controversies Series

Information Age

Social Networking

At Issue Series

Human Embryo Experimentation

Policing the Internet

"Congress shall make
no law ... abridging
the freedom of speech,
or of the press."

First Amendment to the U.S. Constitution

The basic foundation of our democracy is the First Amendment guarantee of freedom of expression. The Opposing Viewpoints series is dedicated to the concept of this basic freedom and the idea that it is more important to practice it than to enshrine it.

OPPOSING
VIEWPOINTS®
SERIES

Technology and Society

David Haugen and Susan Musser, Book Editors

GREENHAVEN PRESS

An imprint of Thomson Gale, a part of The Thomson Corporation

THOMSON

™

GALE

Detroit • New York • San Francisco • New Haven, Conn. • Waterville, Maine • London

Christine Nasso, *Publisher*
Elizabeth Des Chenes, *Managing Editor*

For more information, contact:
Greenhaven Press
27500 Drake Rd.
Farmington Hills, MI 48331-3535
Or you can visit our Internet site at http://www.gale.com

LIBRARY OF CONGRESS CATALOGING-IN-PUBLICATION DATA

Technology and society / David Haugen and Susan Musser, book editors.
    p. cm. -- (Opposing viewpoints)
Includes bibliographical references and index.
ISBN-13: 978-0-7377-3360-0 (hardcover)
ISBN-13: 978-0-7377-3361-7 (pbk.)
  1. Technology--Social aspects. 2. Technological innovations--Social aspects.
3. Technological forecasting. I. Haugen, David M., 1969- II. Musser, Susan.
T14.5.T441678 2007
303.48'3--dc22

                           2007004372

ISBN-10: 0-7377-3360-8 (hardcover)
ISBN-10: 0-7377-3361-6 (pbk.)

Printed in the United States of America
10 9 8 7 6 5 4 3 2 1

Contents

Chapter 3: Should the Government Regulate Technology?

Chapter 4: Will Future Technology Improve Humanity?

Why Consider Opposing Viewpoints?

> *"The only way in which a human being can make some approach to knowing the whole of a subject is by hearing what can be said about it by persons of every variety of opinion and studying all modes in which it can be looked at by every character of mind. No wise man ever acquired his wisdom in any mode but this."*
>
> John Stuart Mill

In our media-intensive culture it is not difficult to find differing opinions. Thousands of newspapers and magazines and dozens of radio and television talk shows resound with differing points of view. The difficulty lies in deciding which opinion to agree with and which "experts" seem the most credible. The more inundated we become with differing opinions and claims, the more essential it is to hone critical reading and thinking skills to evaluate these ideas. Opposing Viewpoints books address this problem directly by presenting stimulating debates that can be used to enhance and teach these skills. The varied opinions contained in each book examine many different aspects of a single issue. While examining these conveniently edited opposing views, readers can develop critical thinking skills such as the ability to compare and contrast authors' credibility, facts, argumentation styles, use of persuasive techniques, and other stylistic tools. In short, the Opposing Viewpoints series is an ideal way to attain the higher-level thinking and reading skills so essential in a culture of diverse and contradictory opinions.

In addition to providing a tool for critical thinking, Opposing Viewpoints books challenge readers to question their own strongly held opinions and assumptions. Most people form their opinions on the basis of upbringing, peer pressure, and personal, cultural, or professional bias. By reading carefully balanced opposing views, readers must directly confront new ideas as well as the opinions of those with whom they disagree. This is not to simplistically argue that everyone who reads opposing views will—or should—change his or her opinion. Instead, the series enhances readers' understanding of their own views by encouraging confrontation with opposing ideas. Careful examination of others' views can lead to the readers' understanding of the logical inconsistencies in their own opinions, perspective on why they hold an opinion, and the consideration of the possibility that their opinion requires further evaluation.

Evaluating Other Opinions

To ensure that this type of examination occurs, Opposing Viewpoints books present all types of opinions. Prominent spokespeople on different sides of each issue as well as well-known professionals from many disciplines challenge the reader. An additional goal of the series is to provide a forum for other, less-known, or even unpopular viewpoints. The opinion of an ordinary person who has had to make the decision to cut off life support from a terminally ill relative, for example, may be just as valuable and provide just as much insight as a medical ethicist's professional opinion. The editors have two additional purposes in including these less-known views. One, the editors encourage readers to respect others' opinions—even when not enhanced by professional credibility. It is only by reading or listening to and objectively evaluating others' ideas that one can determine whether they are worthy of consideration. Two, the inclusion of such viewpoints encourages the important critical thinking skill of objectively evaluating an author's credentials and bias. This evaluation will illuminate an author's reasons for taking a particular stance on an issue and will aid in readers' evaluation of the author's ideas.

It is our hope that these books will give readers a deeper understanding of the issues debated and an appreciation of the complexity of even seemingly simple issues when good and honest people disagree. This awareness is particularly important in a democratic society such as ours in which people enter into public debate to determine the common good. Those with whom one disagrees should not be regarded as enemies but rather as people whose views deserve careful examination and may shed light on one's own.

Thomas Jefferson once said that "difference of opinion leads to inquiry, and inquiry to truth." Jefferson, a broadly educated man, argued that "if a nation expects to be ignorant and free . . . it expects what never was and never will be." As individuals and as a nation, it is imperative that we consider the opinions of others and examine them with skill and discernment. The Opposing Viewpoints series is intended to help readers achieve this goal.

David L. Bender and Bruno Leone,
Founders

Introduction

> *"We can say that any rapid technological advance is always a cause of human disorientation, and that its initial effect is to cause at least almost as much misery as it alleviates. Such change seems to become on balance beneficial only after it becomes routinized, only after it assumes a place in a relatively settled way of life."*
>
> —Peter Augustine Lawler,
> Dana Professor of Government
> at Berry College, Georgia

It is an incontrovertible assessment to claim that technology shapes society, transforming the fundamental ways in which people live, conduct business, travel, communicate, and contemplate the future. Despite the accuracy of this generalization, however, most technological advances are initially available to those who can afford them, and many innovations simply remain out of reach of the poorer segments of society. For most people, doing without certain technologies is acceptable, for the benefits they offer are unnecessary for individuals to survive even in a technologically driven society. Not everyone needs a high-definition television set or an iPod, for example. Yet there are technologies that have so woven their way into the fabric of civilization that few people can do without them.

In a 2003 article for the *Journal of Economic Issues*, Robert E. Prasch, a professor of economics, mentions a couple of these technologies that have become indispensable for the majority of people. Prasch first offers the case of the credit card, asserting:

Not much more than twenty years ago, one could book a plane ticket or hotel room or rent a car by providing a cash deposit. With the diffusion of the credit card, this approach is rarely an option today. In short, for most of us a credit card, considered as a consumer "technology," has become a de facto necessity. Even if one chooses not to borrow against it, it serves as a signifier of trustworthiness, and its widespread use makes its possession a necessity for anyone who wishes to participate in a wide variety of transactions, including transactions that could formerly be conducted without it.

Prasch continues by noting that the poor have a more difficult time obtaining credit cards and typically end up with cards that have higher interest rates because of their insecure incomes. This makes the use of credit cards a more expensive undertaking for those who can least afford it.

As a second example of a requisite technology, Prasch points to the automobile. Cars, he says, have become the dominant mode of transportation, and their rise has signaled the decline of other means of travel that were relatively low-cost, such as trains and trolleys. "Moreover," Prasch writes, "after car ownership became the norm, zoning increasingly separated commercial from residential lands such that access to a dependable automobile is increasingly an implicit or explicit condition of employment. Today a reliable personal vehicle has largely evolved from an option to a necessity."

Prasch argues that the costs of these technologies are a significant burden to the majority of people and most taxing to the poor. He further suggests that newer technologies—especially computer and communications technologies—are following this trend. Using e-mail, Prasch explains, requires the use of a computer, an Internet service provider, and entails other costs for software and upgrades. And in the modern era, individuals are disadvantaged if they do not subscribe to this form of communication. As Prasch succinctly states, "A failure to participate in the world of e-mail effectively excludes one from many, if not virtually all, professional and business activities in contemporary America."

The exclusion of the poor and disadvantaged from the fruits of technological progress in the computer age is the result of what is commonly termed the "digital divide." The digital divide is the gap that separates those with enough money and access to take advantage of technology and those who lack such prerequisites. Just who the have-nots are depends on the demographic under examination. Initially, commentators and critics in the United States placed the divide between the wealthier white segments of society and the poor—mainly black and Hispanic—populations, and most observers still argue that such a divide exists. Writing in *Education Week*, Andrew Trotter reports that the 2000 U.S. census found that 93 percent of white students use computers, while only 86 percent of black students and 86 percent of Hispanic students do. Similarly, Trotter notes that "while 67 percent of white students were likely to use the Internet, just 47 percent of African-American students, 44 percent of Hispanic students, and 58 percent of Asian-American students were likely to do so."

Beyond ethnicity, other demographic factors have more recently been included in defining those disadvantaged by the digital divide. Some researchers, for example, contend that girls are less encouraged to participate in computer learning and Internet technologies, leaving them outpaced by their male counterparts. Others argue that geography itself plays a role in maintaining the divide. Beth Snyder Bulik, writing in a 2006 issue of *Advertising Age*, asserts that technology is more prevalent in big cities than in small towns, chiefly because the manufacturers try to reach the largest, wealthiest market for their products. She states, "In 2005, 62% of rural American adults had Internet access versus 70% of urban adults; that 8 percentage point gap is half what it was just two years ago." Of course, critics maintain that the geographical divisions work on a global scale as well. More industrialized nations such as the United States are centers of digital communication technologies, while developing countries are struggling to acquire and disburse these innovations. In most African countries, for example, less than 1 percent of the population is online, leaving many fearful that the Third World will be excluded from the digital revolution.

Not everyone is convinced that the digital divide is of serious concern. Some critics of the putative crisis have argued that the disadvantaged members of society may not have personal computers from which to participate in the digital age, but they commonly have access to computers at public institutions such as schools and libraries. Others typically assert that while there is a digital divide between haves and have-nots, the gap is not as great as reported and, with the proliferation of cheaper computers, the divide is narrowing. Some also suggest that the unconnected may even choose to be left out. As *Business Week* reporter Amey Stone wrote in 2003, "A good share of the 42% of Americans who don't go online today [in 2003] probably skip the Web due to habit or generational factors. Many are probably among the 31% of Americans who don't use a computer for any reason." Regardless of the holdout, though, independent polls and studies by the Department of Commerce reveal that more people—of all backgrounds—are using computers and going online as never before.

As Prasch suggests, the digital divide—even if not as serious a crisis as some observers believe—is a result of technology becoming dominant, socially integral, and exclusionary. Thus, those who cannot afford technology become further impoverished by their lack of access to the tools needed to participate in, compete in, and enjoy the benefits of an ever-modernizing society. Or, as Prasch warns, "We must . . . become more sensitive to the notion that poverty, in the form of social distance and exclusion, can be induced by technical changes that Western elites find most amenable to their own, somewhat specific, notion of 'the good life.'"

Technologies, then, have a cost, and part of this cost is the obsolescence of older, sometimes cheaper, ways of doing things in order to increase speed, performance, and other measures most sought after by those who can afford the changes. In *Opposing Viewpoints: Technology and Society*, a diverse collection of authors debate the costs and benefits of embracing new technologies in chapters that ask: What Is Technology's Impact on Society? What Impact Does Technology Have on Education? Should the Government Regulate Technology? Will Future Technology Improve Humanity? These analysts address the moral, ethical, and practical aspects of implementing various technologies. All note that these innovations have (or will have) a profound impact on society in general, but implicit in their arguments must be a recognition that many of these technologies—from genetic enhancement to robotics—will likely be concerns primarily for the wealthier classes, who have the time and money to invest in them. In time, though, some of these technologies may become vital for participation in society, leaving the poorer segments struggling to stay connected. "In this sense," Prasch states, "technology can present itself to individuals, and even some communities, as an oppressive force that narrows, rather than expands, the set of choices and ways of life that they may choose."

OPPOSING
VIEWPOINTS®
SERIES

CHAPTER 1

What Is Technology's Impact on Society?

Chapter Preface

In a 2005 article in *Perspectives on Political Science*, Peter Augustine Lawler, a professor of government, argues that technology has been both a boon and a bane to humanity. It has, for example, allowed people to achieve mastery over nature, and it has provided abundance, choice, and opportunity; improved human health and longevity; and even granted a degree of freedom from drudgery and toil. At the same time, Lawler maintains that technology has threatened the normal course of nature, led to the destruction of millions of lives, and—with the development of weapons of mass destruction—put humanity on the brink of self-annihilation.

Lawler contends that balancing the good and bad aspects of technology is becoming more difficult if not impossible because people are so driven by the desire to constantly innovate and build tools to do new things that humanity has lost its perspective on the value of technology. "We find it almost impossible to judge how much and what kind of technology would be best for us," Lawler states. "In principle, we should be free to accept or reject various technological developments. Technology, after all, is supposed to be means for the pursuit of whatever ends we choose. But, in truth, it might be our destiny to be moved along by impersonal and unlimited technological progress."

Each innovation, in Lawler's view, leads to another, and society—which cannot detach itself from this march of progress—has no respite to assess the merits of this advancement. This is, in part, because a technologically driven society desires the order and rationality associated with technological thinking and because it seeks to make this view dominant at the expense of other ways of thinking. In this respect, it devalues introspection and private-interest leisure time as "pointless." Technology—which many have assumed is a means of attaining more time away from work—has, therefore, made leisure impossible. Businesswoman Katharine Giovanni bemoans the fact that a technological society is one that does not allow for rest. In an Internet article, she writes, "Modern technology has taken [relaxation and idleness] away from us. Instead of resting when we get home from work, we work on our laptops and constantly check our PDA's. We take our cell phones and answer them wherever we are . . . in restaurants, airplanes, movie theaters, soccer fields, in our car . . . everywhere!" This slavishness, Giovanni believes, has serious health risks as it strikes against the natural rhythms of the body.

The authors in the following chapter examine the controversial impact of technology on modern society. Some praise technology's evolution for improving work, play, and other qualities of life. Indeed, they look forward to a future in which undreamed-of innovations will progress humanity even further. Others warn of the perils of unquestioningly embracing technology. These critics assert that technology unchallenged may create more problems than it alleviates.

> *"Even with the inherent flaws and growing pains, technology products and services have opened the door to life-changing advances."*

The Benefits of Technology Are Increasing

Jimmy Guterman

In the following viewpoint, Jimmy Guterman analyzes the impact that technology—especially computer technology—has had on American society. Incorporating the opinions of several experts into his review, Guterman reveals that computerized technology has mostly benefited society, from bringing people together via the Internet to increasing people's access to knowledge. Although Guterman acknowledges that technology has fostered some discontent, its advantages have made it integral to the way people work and communicate in the digital age. Jimmy Guterman is the president of the Vineyard Group consulting firm and the publisher and editor of Media Unspun, *an online business newsletter.*

As you read, consider the following questions:

1. In Guterman's assessment, why do people tolerate technologies' imperfections as a part of their daily routines?

2. How has Internet technology improved the quality of people's lives, according to Watts Wacker, as cited by the author?

3. As technology becomes more pervasive, what does Guterman say is the question that "every one of us will have to ask" ourselves and society?

Turn off your MP3 player, even though you just found that pre-release single on Morpheus. Hold off on that Expedia search for cheap fares to Spain. Don't read that e-mail, even if your customized filter tells you it's urgent. Don't enter another appointment into your Palm, and don't answer that cell-phone call, even if it's from your boss. Now is the time to stop and reflect on what technology has done to you. Over the past 20 years, it has gone from merely changing the way Americans get through the day to defining our way of life.

"Everything in America is about technology," says Donald Norman, author of *The Design of Everyday Things* and *The Invisible Computer.* "That's been a symptom of the United States since its foundation. We invented all sorts of crucial technologies: mass production, standardized parts, time zones, you name it."

Though many countries are progressive in their adoption of technology, particularly in Western Europe and Asia, the United States still sets the pace for technological innovation, which can be attributed in part to the same risk-taking, entrepreneurial spirit on which the nation was built. From sequencing the human genome and mapping the universe to altering the rules of war, computing power has not only given us the power to solve some of life's greatest mysteries, it's also made the U.S. a technological hegemony.

Of course, there are two sides to the story. Though technology has gone a long way toward improving our quality of life, it's also raised issues and concerns that give us pause. With that in mind, we saw the 20th Anniversary of *PC Magazine* as an exciting opportunity to explore the impact of the technology, inventions, and products we've been covering since the onset of the PC revolution.

Although the birth of the PC [personal computer] was a great feat, the proliferation of the PC set in motion the most dramatic changes. The continual price drops have led to astounding increases in the computing power that's available to many Americans. In March 1982, when [publishing house] Ziff Davis launched *PC Magazine*, $3,000 would get you a 4.77-MHz single-tasking PC with 64K of memory, no hard drive, and a fuzzy monochrome monitor. Today half as much money can get you a much faster processor, 2,000 times the memory, 300,000 times the storage, and an incalculably superior display.

And of course, there is the Internet. Together the PC and the Internet have been able to bridge enormous physical and social gaps. This dynamic duo has put us on the road to realizing [technology prophet and social critic] Marshall McLuhan's vision of the global village. It has broken down barriers from distance to disability and is considered the Great Leveler—at least by those who have access to it. In 1982, when there was no true commercial Internet, less than 1 percent of American workers had access to the Internet, but today [in 2002] more than half do. Similarly, less than 1 percent of Americans accessed an online service from home, but today more than half of all Americans can connect from home.

Multitasking: The Human Condition

If you used a personal computer 20 years ago, you were among the lucky few who had access to such machines. "In 1982, a normal person didn't use a word processor," says Dan Bricklin, cocreator of the first electronic spreadsheet, VisiCalc. "Computers on the desktop? Not really happening yet in a big way in 1982."

Innovations like the spreadsheet and word processing sparked the PC revolution, putting productivity tools into the hands of many people. And though those tools eased certain tasks, they also shifted the focus from working on a single task to multitasking. Many of us send e-mail, browse the Web, and use a spreadsheet program at the same time. And we've become accustomed to working that way.

"Technology so pervades my life," says Norman. "It all feels like a natural part of my life, except for the 'natural' edges, which I miss. When something is natural, as so much new technology makes many things feel, it seems as though you've been using it forever."

We've even accepted technology's imperfections as a natural part of the deal, no matter how annoying or counterproductive they are. We expect mobile-phone reception to vary, depending on where we're traveling. We expect we'll have to customize printer drivers before we can use our new plug-and-play printers. We expect Windows to crash. Yet we build these time-wasting maneuvers into our daily schedule because of the perceived benefits, but also because technology has changed the way we perceive time.

Esther Dyson, chairman of EDventure Holdings and former editor of the infamous *Release 1.0* newsletter, thinks that this perception is erasing cultural differences, too. "I've seen people's time horizons shorten, especially since September 11, [2001,] although it started well before then," says Dyson. "People want a payoff from what they're doing as soon as possible. I've seen this in both the business and personal realms." She points out that people in the U.S. aren't willing to make appointments, which was similar to what she found in Russia. "When I go to Russia, I say something like, 'Let's meet next Thursday.' A Russian will say, 'Just call me next Wednesday to set it up.'" Dyson attributes the trend in part to technology and in part to the uncertainty of time.

She suggests that this era of pervasive connectivity—in which you have to work hard to keep yourself out of touch—has fundamentally changed the way people operate. "You used to go home and not have any work-related discussion. There wasn't this notion of your boss having immediate access to you," says Dyson. "There was a much stronger division between work and home until computers came along."

The separation between work and home is certainly gone for Eric Raymond, who doesn't mind one bit. Raymond, one of the most public voices in the open-source movement and author of the seminal essay "The Cathedral and the Bazaar," appreciates his inability to tell the difference between his work and personal life. "The closest thing I've had to a vacation in the past five years was a 'geek cruise.' The ship was filled with Linux geeks there for a technical conference. I had a really good time. It fulfilled the traditional vacation needs, but my work is my recreation," says Raymond. "Technology makes it easier to do that. The people on that cruise were my community."

That's one of the most dramatic changes technology has brought over the past 20 years: the opportunity to share in new ways and create communities based on common interests, without geography getting in the way. If you want to correspond and trade music with the world's biggest Otis Redding fan, it doesn't matter whether she lives in the next town or the next continent. Raymond didn't need a "geek cruise" to connect with his peers in a meaningful way; he's been doing that for many years through e-mail and newsgroup postings.

Similarly, Watts Wacker, CEO and futurist for FirstMatter, firmly believes that technology—especially with the advent of the Internet—has improved the quality of life over the past 20 years. "People used to have only a few deep relationships in their lifetimes. Now people have a great many deep relationships that last nanoseconds," says Wacker. "It adds up to a different expression of self. Personal computers have been that transformative. Think about Napster [a site offering downloadable music]. Because of Napster, 100 million people were doing something that couldn't have been done previously. This is a harbinger for fundamental shifts in [our] social agenda that the Net will continue to bring. Something about the online experience has tapped into the human condition."

Many people agree with Wacker about this tech-inspired integration being a good thing—mostly. "In an industrial society, the thinking has been that either you're slaving on the assembly line or you're at home," says Jakob Nielsen, Donald Norman's partner at the user-experience consultancy firm, the Nielsen Norman Group, and author of *Designing Web Usability*. "Before that, people were surrounded by their work—living in their work. That says something about human nature. Maybe our business and personal lives are all meant to flow together on some level."

Can't Leave Home Without It

PCs with Internet connections are pervasive, but perhaps not to the same degree as mobile phones. Cellular communication is even more entrenched than PCs: There are at least three times as many mobile phones operating in the U.S. today as computers, according to IDC [technology market advisory firm]. Although the trend is to make mobile phones more like computers as they take on more computing and data-transfer tasks, most people in the U.S. use them for one thing: to keep in touch. And like computer use, mobile-phone usage raises new sociological questions. (It doesn't help that Dockers just released a line of Mobile Pants, into which we can stuff mobile phones, PDAs, and pagers.)

"Cell phones are weird," Norman says. "Look at people who take cell phone calls in the middle of the street and go into a trancelike state. They have left where they are physically

The Pleasures of Progress

Technology represents man's attempt to make life easier. Technological advances improve people's standard of living, increase leisure time, help eliminate poverty, and lead to a greater variety of products. Progress allows people more time to spend on higher-level concerns such as character development, love, religion, and the perfection of one's soul.

If people resisted technological change, they would be expressing their satisfaction with existing levels of disease, hunger, and privation. In addition, without experimentation and change, human existence would be boring; human fulfillment is dependent on novelty, surprise, and creativity.

An innovative idea from one man not only contributes to the progress of others, but also creates conditions permitting people to advance even further. Ideas interact in unexpected ways, and innovations are frequently used in unforeseen applications. Technological progress involves a series of stages consisting of experimentation, competition, errors, and feedback.

Edward W. Younkins, Freeman, *January 2000.*

and focused on interacting with the person on the telephone. That's fascinating, but the problem is that people are not having this experience privately. Voice knows no spatial boundaries. Others are forced to participate."

In other words, technology is everywhere we are, regardless of whether we want it there or not, and it has caused some public outcry and some lawmakers to spring into action to set boundaries; several states have banned cell phone use while driving, for example. As technology continues to invade our lives, the question every one of us will have to ask is where to draw the line. Just because we can bring our 3-pound subnotebooks with us on vacation, should we? Just because we can get e-mail piped into our car, should we? These questions aren't as profound as the ethical questions scientists must answer as technology offers potentially life-altering knowledge, but they do illustrate the need to stop and consider the implications.

Many people welcome the arrival of technology where it wasn't before. As the inventor of Ethernet and founder of 3Com, Bob Metcalfe has either conceived or had early access to new technologies. But for Metcalfe, the technology that gets him down the road—literally—gets his rave reviews. "The navigational system in my car has been a life-changing technology for me," says Metcalfe, who now serves as a general partner at the venture-capital firm Polaris Venture Partners.

"The system tells me where to go," says Metcalfe. "It has a female voice, so I named her Sadie. Sadie annoys my wife, because she tells me to prepare to turn when I'm talking to my wife." But now Metcalfe is fearless. He takes his son to play hockey all over New England. He just punches in the address, and Sadie takes him there. "Five times this week I've been delighted when Sadie found me a shorter way to get somewhere," says Metcalfe. "She's not perfect, but I trust her. I'm being taught the geography of New England by my car. That's an amazing thing for technology to do."

Should You Take Technology to Bed?

Where will technology sneak in next? As computers spread throughout the country and throughout our homes, they have given us the luxury—and for some, the headache—of instant access to information. "For a while we had a computer in the dining room," says Norman. "We'd talk during dinner, a question would come up, and we'd get an answer, then come right back to the dinner table. For those sorts of things, a computer was better than a dictionary."

For other people, the constant presence of a PC causes conflict, however. "My husband and I have this ongoing fight over whether the computer is allowed in the bedroom," says Brenda Laurel, founder of landmark girl-game company Purple Moon and author of *Utopian Entrepreneur*. "As far as I'm concerned, the bedroom is a no-computing zone unless someone is injured. I want a vacation from technology every night when we go to bed. My husband [a scientist for AT&T Labs] loves to hack, but I don't want him doing that in the bedroom. So far, I'm winning the fight."

Laurel says she does know people who take their computers to bed with them, and they're not necessarily bad people, but that strikes her as a place that should be off-limits. "At some point, you have to live without technology. Almost every day you see someone using technology in a way that intrudes on someone else's life."

That's not to say that Laurel, who has been thinking about the effects of technology on behavior at least since her stint at the Atari Sunnyvale Research Lab in the early 1980s, wants to label some sites off-limits to all technology. "When my husband and I flew to Phoenix to see a meteor shower, we took our GPS with us, so we wouldn't get lost, but we didn't take our cell phones. I guess it's a matter of deciding which technologies are appropriate and which aren't."

Laurel acknowledges that technology has changed her life but that the biggest change has been through her kids. "Last year we got them each an iBook. I am surprised that they use them constantly for school as research tools. When I see them walking around with their iBooks, I wonder how my life would have been different had I had access to such technology as a child."

"In many ways, you can't grow up without a PC now," says Bricklin. "You must have a laptop if you want to attend many colleges." Today PCs are an accepted part of education, even for younger kids. Twenty years ago, a child was presented with a computer in an educational setting to teach the child to program, says Bricklin. Not anymore. "Right now you have a generation of Americans growing up who can't imagine life without PCs, in the same way that the previous generation couldn't imagine a world without telephones or automobiles."

Just as Norman takes for granted that his house knows what temperature he likes and Metcalfe is increasingly comfortable handing over control in his car to Sadie, Bricklin sees current and future generations assuming that computers can do many things better than people. "Google is a good example," he says. "There's a growing acceptance that something like Google is the best way to find information. And everything has to be on the Web. We expect everyone to have Web sites, and we're frustrated when someone doesn't. Something like that was completely unheard of 20 years ago." Metcalfe adds, "Having a Web site now is like having a telex number 20 years ago. It's something you had to have." But he acknowledges, "Unlike the Web, there wasn't much you could do with a telex other than take orders."

The more you hear Bricklin talk about what PCs have wrought, the more you sense that he's still a tremendous optimist. "You look at old spy flicks, all those James Bond movies, and you see the heroes all had these amazing skills, more than anyone could have. It's not like that in 2002. Now we're giving the average person greater capabilities and raising the level of what they can get done. At their best, PCs free people to do more interesting work. They have improved people's lives in many subtle and not-so-subtle ways."

"There's a negative story as well," contends Nielsen. "You could argue that technology has made us far more reactive, made us multitask more, and made it harder to be thoughtful, sit down, and just do a project. Now, thanks to technology, you have 20 tasks you have to do at the same time. You have all these windows open, all these e-mails and instant messages to respond to right away. So many of these new applications are more disruptive than helpful. We're still only partway through the transformations that PCs will bring to us, and many of them will be good."

Meanwhile, there is still the issue of a digital divide in America—one that exacerbates other divides, economic and otherwise, in American culture. There are still thousands of households in the U.S. without a computer. It's great that inner-city fifth graders who never had access to computers can now run Bank Street Writer on their handed-down PC ATs, but children in the private school a couple blocks away are using Mathematica and Photoshop every day and are starting the ladder many rungs higher. In a time when some schools have trouble finding the money to pay for staplers, issues like Windows XP compatibility and broadband security still seem far away. Many kids are still getting left behind, especially as the high end of computing gets higher and higher.

The good news is that people without home computers are seeking them out in other locations, such as friends' homes, libraries, community centers, and Internet cafés. And they are increasingly adopting other types of technology, such as pagers and cell phones.

Technology in America is full of contradictions. We use technology to collect travel information, so we can go to a place where technology can't reach us. We spend countless hours customizing and synchronizing the personal digital assistants intended to save us time. And there's the productivity lost to too many open windows, PC reboots, and voice mail bounces. But none of us are considering discarding our devices, sharpening our pencils, or unplugging our networks. Even with the inherent flaws and growing pains, technology products and services have opened the door to life-changing advances. And even if we did discard our devices, we'd use technology to do that, too. (Hello, eBay.)

Technology in America. Though a tremendous improvement over where it was 20 years ago, technology is likely nothing compared with what it will be 20 years from now. Will [the computer] industry solve today's pressing usability and distraction issues? What new problems will emerge as side effects of new technologies? What unthinkable advance is about to change how you live your life? What will demand your attention next? Stay tuned.

> "Never before in the human story has so much frenetic innovation delivered so little of real worth."

The Benefits of Technology are Diminishing

David Cox

David Cox is a writer and television producer in the United Kingdom. In the following article, Cox claims that significant technological innovation is in decline. Instead, the modern world, in his view, is plagued with purposeless technologies that distract people from the realization that progress is slowing. More importantly, Cox maintains, humanity's misplaced faith in continual advancement has created an overreliance on technology that blinds people to its dangers.

As you read, consider the following questions:

1. What basic man-made elements of modern civilization have not changed much over time, according to Cox?
2. As reported by the author, in what year does Jonathan Huebner believe technological inventiveness reached a peak?

3. What technological advances does Cox say may be unwittingly contributing to human suffering?

Looking back on the [December holiday] festivities, do you perhaps feel Santa let you down? Maybe your son's £90 Roboraptor is already lying abandoned, its state-of-the-art animatronics no match for the comforting, one-eyed gaze of his tattered old teddy. Does your daughter find her £150, radio-controlled X-UFO as much fun as that paper kite you picked up for her in the market?

And what about your own quad-band, polyphonic, game-savvy, video-capture, zoom-equipped camphone? Can you be bothered to find out what its cutting-edge features do, let alone actually use them?

You could be forgiven for concluding that the challenge of Christmas proved too much for 21st-century technology. Perhaps you wish you'd stuck with socks and scarves. However, your irritation may not stop there. Has a flattened TV screen or bagless vacuum cleaner actually enhanced your life? Do you really need sat-nav [GPS], a portable video player or a vibrating head massager?

False Promises of Updated Technology

Never before in the human story has so much frenetic innovation delivered so little of real worth. Hucksters ceaselessly imply that unless we update our kit, our lives will lose their lustre. Yet usually, rather than teleportation, eternal youth or silent popcorn, the most they can deliver is a slightly faster, slightly smaller or slightly fancier version of what we already have. Sometimes it is actually inferior.

You probably didn't expect digital radio to sound worse than FM, though you may have noticed that MP3 is no match for CDs, which in turn sound less impressive than your dad's black vinyl discs. And guess what, vinyl records are coming back into favour among the discriminating classes, along with bicycles, fountain pens, coal fires and candles.

We remain convinced that ours is an age of breakneck technological progress, yet most of the things we rely on, such as cars, planes and houses, have barely changed in their essentials since our grandparents' day. Our enemies sidestep our high-tech weapons systems with backpack bombs, while medicine is still humbled by cancer and the common cold.

The advances of our era may be numerous, but few match up in scale to the triumphs of the past. We preen ourselves about the internet, but the most profound insights on which it depends occurred long ago and had already found expression in arguably far more important inventions such as the library and the telephone. Certainly, the web pales in comparison with the printing press, which in turn pales in comparison with writing. What discovery in our own lifetimes can match fire or language, the wheel or the boat, agriculture or the city?

Inventiveness in Decline

Recently, a Pentagon physicist called Jonathan Huebner decided to try to plot the rate at which the level of innovation has been changing. He devised a mathematical formula to calculate the number of significant developments per head of population. By this measure, our current score is about the same as it would have been in 1600. It turns out that in modern times inventiveness peaked in 1873, and since then has been declining steadily. By 2024 it should be back to a level last experienced in the Dark Ages.

We need not be surprised. The low-hanging fruit of spectacular intuition was harvested long ago.

Sadly, the iron law of diminishing returns prevents any latter-day Leonardo from achieving half a dozen breakthroughs in unrelated fields in a single lifetime. Nowadays, a small step forward requires huge teams, which must first absorb an immense backlog of relevant data. By the time they have done this, many will be in the final stages of their careers, and this spawns a further problem.

The Paradox of Technological Progress

Technology is a problem because we cannot do without it and our use of it clearly makes us both better and worse. Human beings are—among other things—technological or tool-making animals. We use our brains and our freedom to transform nature, and in doing so we transform ourselves. We also have a perverse capacity to make ourselves unhappy and a singular pride in our misery. We are both proud of and wish to free ourselves from the burdens of our technological success. So we find it almost impossible to judge how much and what kind of technology would be best for us. In principle, we should be free to accept or reject various technological developments. Technology, after all, is supposed to be means for the pursuit of whatever ends we choose. But, in truth, it might be our destiny to be moved along by impersonal and unlimited technological progress. We do not have much evidence of significant numbers of human beings resisting technological changes for long periods of time. (The peaceful and admirable Amish, for example, are a very small exception to a general rule.)

Peter Augustine Lawler, Perspectives on Political Science, *Summer 2005.*

The Dangers of Progress

Creative energy is firmly associated with youth. We are rightly impressed by the wizardry of the teenage geeks who devise the computer viruses that make our lives hell. Unfortunately, the structure of the research and development process today means that by the time such people are in a position to contribute something more useful, their genius may well have evaporated.

Where significant headway does get made, it is often in areas which have become so complex that further effort makes no economic sense. Thus, space exploration has more or less been abandoned. And there's an even more awesome block to continued progress. Many of the discoveries that remain to be made may be just too complex for the human brain ever to absorb.

Still, you may ask, if faith in our technological prowess is misplaced, why should it matter? A disappointing Christmas present isn't the end of the world. Unfortunately, rather more than that may be at stake. Over-reliance on technology could turn out to be the death of us.

The darker side of our endless search for cleverer stuff is becoming increasingly apparent. It's our enthusiasm for air travel that may enable what might otherwise be localised diseases such as AIDS, TB, SARS or bird flu to kill us in our millions. Reliance on genetically modified crops could result in mass starvation if things go wrong. The Heir [Britain's Prince Charles] fears that nanotechnology may reduce us all to grey goo. Apparently, a mistake by some over-eager physicist in some obscure laboratory might even set in motion a chain of events that could destroy all the matter in the universe.

These, however, are mere possibilities. Technophilia creates other perils that now seem inescapable. For one thing, it encourages us to cling to a way of life predicated on economic growth, which assumes continuing innovation on a scale that may fail to materialise. It also fosters the delusion that ingenuity can sort out all our problems, which in turn disinclines us to apply the more realistic remedies that may be what we actually require.

Misplaced Faith in Technology

As it happens, our current civilisation is confronting a nexus of difficulties perhaps more daunting than anything faced by its predecessors, and our technological excesses have to bear at least some of the blame. Squandering the colossal bounty of fossilised carbon in a few generations may turn out to have been our main mistake, but it was our otherwise rather unimpressive machines that made this possible.

All the same, the White House is not alone in trusting to technology to come up with a fix for global warming. At some level, the same conviction underpins resistance everywhere else to the understandably unwelcome alternative—an adjustment of our appetites. The thinking seems to be that if we were clever enough to create such a mess, we must be clever enough to get ourselves out of it.

Finding a replacement for fossil fuels, should we manage to survive until they have run out, is also apparently to be left largely to our inventiveness. Many of us seem to be cheerily assuming that if nuclear power turns out to be too expensive or too dangerous, our limitless cunning will in due course tease some other genie from some other lamp. Unfortunately, the panto season [i.e., the time of playacting] has not much longer to run.

Meanwhile, as our nemesis creeps up on us, we are reduced to revisiting long-abandoned contrivances from less hubristic eras. The windmills flailing anew above our landscape should be seen as signalling the limits of our capabilities. We might as well look to Santa to safeguard our destiny as to our power over wind and waves. He may of course disappoint us, as perhaps he did this Christmas, but at least we realise that we're not supposed to believe in him.

> "People not only socialize online, but they also incorporate the internet into seeking information, exchanging advice, and making decisions."

The Internet Connects People

Jeffrey Boase et al.

Jeffrey Boase was a doctoral student in the Department of Sociology at the University of Toronto in Canada when this viewpoint was written. In the service of the Pew Internet & American Life Project (a nonprofit think tank that researches the impact of the Internet on American life), Boase and his associates compiled the results of two national surveys that examined the effect of the Internet upon the social networks and relationships of individual participants. The following viewpoint is the researchers' summary of these results. According to Boase and his colleagues, the Internet has facilitated interpersonal contacts among friends and close relations while broadening users' social networks to include people from all over the world with shared interests.

As you read, consider the following questions:

1. What are the two types of interpersonal ties examined in the Pew surveys, and what is the difference between the two?

Jeffrey Boase et al., "The Strength of Internet Ties," Pew Internet & American Life Project, January 5, 2006. Reproduced by permission.

2. What explanations do Boase and his colleagues offer to make sense of their finding that e-mail correspondence does not decline as the size of a person's social network increases?

3. What is "media mutiplexity" as defined by the authors?

Editor's note: this article contains Pew Internet & American Life findings.

Once upon a time, the internet was seen as something special, available only to wizards and geeks. Now it has become part of everyday life. People routinely integrate it into the ways in which they communicate with each other, moving between phone, computer, and in-person encounters.

Our evidence calls into question fears that social relationships—and community—are fading away in America. Instead of disappearing, people's communities are transforming: The traditional human orientation to neighborhood- and village-based groups is moving towards communities that are oriented around geographically dispersed social networks. People communicate and maneuver in these networks rather than being bound up in one solitary community. Yet people's networks continue to have substantial numbers of relatives and neighbors—the traditional bases of community—as well as friends and workmates.

The internet and email play an important role in maintaining these dispersed social networks. Rather than conflicting with people's community ties, we find that the internet fits seamlessly with in-person and phone encounters. With the help of the internet, people are able to maintain active contact with sizable social networks, even though many of the people in those networks do not live nearby. Moreover, there is media multiplexity: The more that people see each other in person and talk on the phone, the more they use the internet. The connectedness that the internet and other media foster within social networks has real payoffs: People use the internet to seek out others in their networks of contacts when they need help.

Networked Individualism

Because individuals—rather than households—are separately connected, the internet and the cell phone have transformed communication from house-to-house to person-to-person. This creates a new basis for community that author Barry Wellman [one of the authors of this report] has called "*networked individualism*": Rather than relying on a single community for social capital, individuals often must actively seek out a variety of appropriate people and resources for different situations.

While traditional means of communications such as in-person visits and landline telephone conversations are the primary ways by which people keep up with those in their social networks, our research shows that email helps people cultivate social networks. We find that email supplements, rather than replaces, the communication people have with people who are very close to them—as well as with those not so close. Email is especially important to those who have large social networks.

In a social environment based on networked individualism, the internet's capacity to help maintain and cultivate social networks has real payoffs. Our work shows that internet use provides online Americans a path to resources, such as access to people who may have the right information to help deal with a health or medical issue or to confront a financial issue. Sometimes this assistance comes from a close friend or family member. Sometimes this assistance comes from a person more socially distant, but made close by email in a time of need. The result is that people not only socialize online, but they also incorporate the internet into seeking information, exchanging advice, and making decisions. . . .

Maintaining Connections and Close Relationships

This report is built primarily around findings of a survey conducted in February 2004 that we call the Social Ties survey. It focused on the nature and scope of people's social networks, how they use their social networks to get help, and how they use information and communication technology.

The Social Ties survey asked about two types of connections people have in their social networks:

- Core Ties: These are the people in Americans' social networks with whom they have very close relationships—the people to whom Americans turn to discuss important matters, with whom they are in frequent contact, or from whom they seek help. This approach captures three key dimensions of relationship strength—emotional intimacy, contact, and the availability of social network capital.

- Significant Ties: These are the people outside that ring of "core ties" in Americans' social networks, who are somewhat closely connected. They are the ones with whom Americans to a lesser extent discuss important matters, are in less frequent contact, and are less apt to seek help. They may do some or all of these things, but to a lesser extent. Nevertheless, although significant ties are weaker than core ties, they are more than acquaintances, and they can become important players at times as people access their networks to get help or advice.

Americans connect with their core and significant ties in a variety of ways. They continue to use in-person encounters and landline telephones. Yet new communication technologies—email, cell phones, and instant messaging (IM)—now play important roles in connecting network members. The in-

The Growing Role of the Internet in Decision-Making

Number of Americans for which Internet was crucial or important

	2005	2002
Gotten additional training for your career	21 million	14 million
Helped another person with a major illness or medical condition	17	11
Chosen a school or college for yourself or your child	17	12
Bought a car	16	13
Made a major investment or financial decision	16	11
Found a new place to live	10	7
Changed jobs	8	7
Dealt yourself with a major illness or other health condition	7	5

The margin of error ±3% for the sample of internet users in both surveys.

TAKEN FROM: Jeffrey Boase et al., "The Strength of Internet Ties," Pew Internet & American Life Project, January 5, 2006.

ternet does not stand alone but as part of an overall communication system in which people use many means to communicate.

Regular Contact through E-mail

As the size of a person's social network increases, it becomes more difficult for people to contact a large percentage of network members. This makes intuitive sense. If you have 50 people in your social network, it will take a fair amount of effort to contact 25 of them regularly by using the telephone. If your social network is 20 people in size, it will take less effort to contact 15 of them regularly. Even though there are fewer people contacted, they are a greater percentage of your network.

This pattern—the percentage of one's social network contacted declining as network size grows—holds true for almost all forms of contact analyzed in the Social Ties survey. The one exception is email. As the size of people's social network increases, the percentage of one's social network contacted weekly by email does not decline but remains about the same at about 20% of core and significant ties.

Several qualities of email help make sense of these findings. Email enables people to maintain more relationships easily because of its convenience as a communication tool and the control it gives in managing communication. Email's asynchronous nature—the ability for people to carry on conversations at different times and at their leisure—makes it possible for a quick note to an associate, whether it is about important news or seeking advice on an important decision. Moreover, it is almost as easy to email a message to many people as it is to email to only one. . . .

Contrary to fears that email would reduce other forms of contact, there is "media multiplexity": The more contact by email, the more in-person and phone contact. As a result, Americans are probably more in contact with members of their communities and social networks than before the advent of the internet.

- People who email the vast majority (80%–100%) of their core ties weekly are in phone contact with 25% more of their core ties than non-emailers. Moreover, those who email the vast majority of their significant ties weekly are in phone contact with twice as many of their significant ties than non-emailers.

- The patterns are somewhat different for in-person contact. Those who email the vast majority of their core ties weekly see the same percentage of their core ties weekly as do non-emailers. However, those who email the vast majority of their significant ties weekly do see 50% more of their significant ties weekly than non-emailers.

Getting Help with Important Issues

The February 2004 Social Ties survey asked respondents whether they have sought help from people in their social networks pertaining to eight specific key issues in their lives. The eight issues are:

- Caring for someone with a major illness or medical condition
- Looking for information about a major illness or medical condition
- Making a major investment or financial decision
- Finding a new place to live
- Changing jobs
- Buying a personal computer
- Putting up drywall in your house
- Deciding who to vote for in an election

Most Americans (81%) have asked for help with one of these issues from at least one of their core ties, while nearly half (46%) have asked for help with one of these issues from at least one of their significant ties.

Internet users are more likely than non-users to receive help from core network members: 85% of online users have received help with at least one of the eight issues as compared with 72% of non-users. The average internet user received help on 3.1 of the eight issues from people in their core networks, compared with non-users getting help for 2.0 topics. . . .

Using the Internet to Face Life-Changing Events

When the Social Ties Survey showed that people use the internet to activate their social networks when they need help, we followed up in a survey in March 2005 that we call the Major Moments survey. In it we asked Americans if they had faced any of eight different decisions or milestones in their lives in the previous two years. Nearly a third (29%) of American adults said the internet had played a crucial or important role in helping them sort through their options for at least one of the decisions—and some had gone through several of them. Overall, that represents about 60 million adults. The eight major decisions queried in the survey were these:

- Getting additional training for your career: About 21 million said the internet had played a crucial or important role in this.

- Helping another person with a major illness or medical condition*: About 17 million said the internet had played a crucial or important role in this.

- Choosing a school for yourself or a child: About 17 million said the internet had played a crucial or important role in this.

- Buying a car: About 16 million said the internet had played a crucial or important role in this.

- Making a major investment or financial decision*: About 16 million said the internet had played a crucial or important role in this.

- Finding a new place to live*: About 10 million said the internet had played a crucial or important role in this.

- Changing jobs*: About 8 million said the internet had played a crucial or important role in this.

- Dealing oneself with a major illness or health condition*: About 7 million said the internet had played a crucial or important role in this.

(The asterisks mark the five events that were queried in both the Social Ties and Major Moments surveys.)

When the Pew Internet Project conducted a survey in January 2002 on the same eight life decision points, 45 million adult Americans said then that the internet had played a crucial or important role in at least one of the decisions.

> *"Heavy use of the Net can actually iso-*
> *late younger socially connected people."*

The Internet Isolates People

Brent Staples

In the following viewpoint, New York Times *editorial writer Brent Staples argues that Internet use can deprive people—especially young people—of cultivating interpersonal skills. He contends that online activities are solitary experiences and that electronic communications have none of the socializing rewards of face-to-face encounters. In Staples's view, overuse of the Internet can lead to disruptions in family relationships and retard the personal growth that comes from learning how to interact with others in the real world.*

As you read, consider the following questions:

1. In Staples's view, who has benefited the most from Internet communication?

2. As the author reports, by what percent does direct contact with family members drop for every hour one spends online?

3. As reported by Staples, who is Marcus Arnold and what did he do to bring himself notoriety?

My 10th-grade heartthrob was the daughter of a fearsome steelworker who struck terror into the hearts of 15-year-old boys. He made it his business to answer the telephone—and so always knew who was calling—and grumbled in the background when the conversation went on too long. Unable to make time by phone, the boy either gave up or appeared at the front door. This meant submitting to the intense scrutiny that the girl's father soon became known for.

He greeted me with a crushing handshake, then leaned in close in a transparent attempt to find out whether I was one of those bad boys who smoked. He retired to the den during the visit, but cruised by the living room now and then to let me know he was watching. He let up after some weeks, but only after getting across what he expected of a boy who spent time with his daughter and how upset he'd be if I disappointed him.

This was my first sustained encounter with an adult outside my family who needed to be convinced of my worth as a person. This, of course, is a crucial part of growing up. Faced with same challenge today, however, I would probably pass on meeting the girl's father—and outflank him on the Internet.

Cutting Out Face-to-Face Encounters

Thanks to e-mail, online chat rooms and instant messages—which permit private, real-time conversations—adolescents have at last succeeded in shielding their social lives from adult scrutiny. But this comes at a cost: teenagers nowadays are both more connected to the world at large than ever, and more cut off from the social encounters that have historically prepared young people for the move into adulthood.

The Internet was billed as a revolutionary way to enrich our social lives and expand our civic connections. This seems to have worked well for elderly people and others who were isolated before they got access to the World Wide Web. But a growing body of research is showing that heavy use of the Net

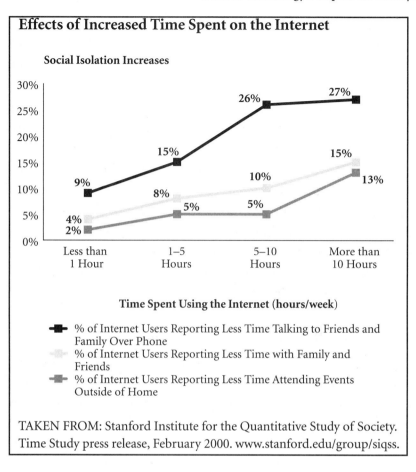

Effects of Increased Time Spent on the Internet

Social Isolation Increases

Time Spent Using the Internet (hours/week)

- % of Internet Users Reporting Less Time Talking to Friends and Family Over Phone
- % of Internet Users Reporting Less Time with Family and Friends
- % of Internet Users Reporting Less Time Attending Events Outside of Home

TAKEN FROM: Stanford Institute for the Quantitative Study of Society. Time Study press release, February 2000. www.stanford.edu/group/siqss.

can actually isolate younger socially connected people who unwittingly allow time online to replace face-to-face interactions with their families and friends.

Online shopping, checking e-mail and Web surfing—mainly solitary activities—have turned out to be more isolating than watching television, which friends and family often do in groups. Researchers have found that the time spent in direct contact with family members drops by as much as half for every hour we use the Net at home.

This should come as no surprise to the two-career couples who have seen their domestic lives taken over by e-mail and wireless tethers that keep people working around the clock.

But a startling body of research from the Human-Computer Interaction Institute at Carnegie Mellon [University] has shown that heavy Internet use can have a stunting effect outside the home as well.

Studies show that gregarious, well-connected people actually lost friends, and experienced symptoms of loneliness and depression, after joining discussion groups and other activities. People who communicated with disembodied strangers online found the experience empty and emotionally frustrating but were nonetheless seduced by the novelty of the new medium. As Prof. Robert Kraut, a Carnegie Mellon researcher, told me recently, such people allowed low-quality relationships developed in virtual reality to replace higher-quality relationships in the real world.

The Substitute World of Cyberspace

No group has embraced this socially impoverishing trade-off more enthusiastically than adolescents, many of whom spend most of their free hours cruising the Net in sunless rooms. This hermetic existence has left many of these teenagers with nonexistent social skills—a point widely noted in stories about the computer geeks who rose to prominence in the early days of Silicon Valley.

Adolescents are drawn to cyberspace for different reasons than adults. As the writer Michael Lewis observed in his book *Next: The Future Just Happened*, children see the Net as a transformational device that lets them discard quotidian identities for more glamorous ones. Mr. Lewis illustrated the point with Marcus Arnold, who, as a 15-year-old, adopted a pseudonym a few years ago and posed as a 25-year-old legal expert for an Internet information service. Marcus did not feel the least bit guilty, and wasn't deterred, when real-world lawyers discovered his secret and accused him of being a fraud. When asked whether he had actually read the law, Marcus responded

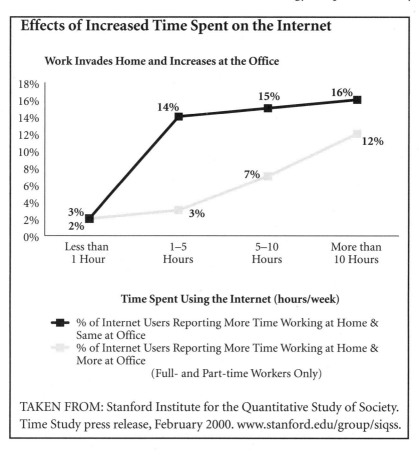

Effects of Increased Time Spent on the Internet

Work Invades Home and Increases at the Office

Time Spent Using the Internet (hours/week)

■ % of Internet Users Reporting More Time Working at Home & Same at Office

▦ % of Internet Users Reporting More Time Working at Home & More at Office

(Full- and Part-time Workers Only)

TAKEN FROM: Stanford Institute for the Quantitative Study of Society. Time Study press release, February 2000. www.stanford.edu/group/siqss.

that he found books "boring," leaving us to conclude that he had learned all he needed to know from his family's big-screen TV.

Marcus is a child of the Net, where everyone has a pseudonym, telling a story makes it true, and adolescents create older, cooler, more socially powerful selves any time they wish. The ability to slip easily into a new, false self is tailor-made for emotionally fragile adolescents, who can consider a bout of acne or a few excess pounds an unbearable tragedy.

But teenagers who spend much of their lives hunched over computer screens miss the socializing, the real-world experience that would allow them to leave adolescence behind and grow into adulthood. These vital experiences, like much else, are simply not available in a virtual form.

> *"We are about to see a seismic shift in the American workforce."*

Robots Are Replacing People

Marshall Brain

Marshall Brain is an author, speaker, and founder of the How Stuff Works Web site. In the following viewpoint, Brain contends that modern automated kiosks are the first wave of robots to enter the world's workforce. He predicts that subsequent incarnations of robots will appear more human and take on more and more human responsibilities. Brain foresees that by 2055 most jobs—in service fields, construction, and administration—will be handled by robots, and that the consequence of this automation will be massive human unemployment.

As you read, consider the following questions:

1. In what year does Brain predict all fast-food meals will be ordered from an automated kiosk?
2. How many human jobs does the author think will be lost to robots by 2015?
3. What invention analogy does Brain use to show the inevitability of robots' transformation of American society?

I went to McDonald's this weekend with the kids. We go to McDonald's to eat about once a week because it is a mile from the house and has an indoor play area. Our normal routine is to walk in to McDonald's, stand in line, order, stand around waiting for the order, sit down, eat and play.

On Sunday, this decades-old routine changed forever. When we walked in to McDonald's, an attractive woman in a suit greeted us and said, "Are you planning to visit the play area tonight?" The kids screamed, "Yeah!" "McDonald's has a new system that you can use to order your food right in the play area. Would you like to try it?" The kids screamed, "Yeah!"

The woman walks us over to a pair of kiosks in the play area. She starts to show me how the kiosks work and the kids scream, "We want to do it!" So I pull up a chair and the kids stand on it while the (extremely patient) woman in a suit walks the kids through the screens. David ordered his food, Irena ordered her food, I ordered my food. It's a simple system. Then it was time to pay. Interestingly, the kiosk only took cash in the form of bills. So I fed my bills into the machine. Then you take a little plastic number to set on your table and type the number in. The transaction is complete.

We sat down at a table. We put our number in the center of the table and waited. In about 10 seconds the kids screamed, "When is our food going to get here???" I said, "Let's count." In less than two minutes a woman in an apron put a tray with our food on the table, handed us our change, took the plastic number and left.

You know what? It is a nice system. It works. It is much nicer than standing in line. The only improvement I would request is the ability to use a credit card.

I will make this prediction: by 2008, every meal in every fast food restaurant will be ordered from a kiosk like this, or from a similar system embedded in each table.

As nice as this system is, however, I think that it represents the tip of an iceberg that we do not understand. This iceberg is going to change the American economy in ways that are very hard to imagine.

Robots Are Here

The iceberg looks like this. On that same day, I interacted with five different automated systems like the kiosks in McDonald's:

- I got money in the morning from the ATM.
- I bought gas from an automated pump.
- I bought groceries at BJ's (a warehouse club) using an extremely well-designed self-service checkout line.
- I bought some stuff for the house at Home Depot using their not-as-well-designed-as-BJ's self-service checkout line.
- I bought my food at McDonald's at the kiosk, as described above.

All of these systems are very easy-to-use from a customer standpoint, they are fast, and they lower the cost of doing business and should therefore lead to lower prices. All of that is good, so these automated systems will proliferate rapidly.

The problem is that these systems will also eliminate jobs in massive numbers. In fact, we are about to see a seismic shift in the American workforce. As a nation, we have no way to understand or handle the level of unemployment that we will see in our economy over the next several decades.

Vision of the Future

These kiosks and self-service systems are the beginning of the robotic revolution. When most people think about robots, they think about independent, autonomous, talking robots like the ones we see in science fiction films. C-3PO and R2-D2 are powerful robotic images that have been around for decades. Robots like these will come into our lives much more quickly than we imagine—self-service checkout systems are the first primitive signs of the trend. Here is one view from the future to show you where we are headed:

"The robot won it again!"

Automated retail systems like ATMs, kiosks and self-service checkout lines marked the beginning of the robotic revolution. Over the course of fifteen years starting in 2001, these systems proliferated and evolved until nearly every retail transaction could be handled in an automated way. Five million jobs in the retail sector were lost as a result of these systems.

The next step was autonomous, humanoid robots. The mechanics of walking were not simple, but Honda had proven that those problems could be solved with the creation of its ASIMO robot at the turn of the century. Sony and other manufacturers followed Honda's lead. Over the course of two decades, engineers refined this hardware and the software controlling it to the point where they could create humanoid bodyforms with the grace and precision of a ballerina or the mass and sheer strength of the Incredible Hulk.

Decades of research and development work on autonomous robotic intelligence finally started to pay off. By 2025, the first machines that could see, hear, move and manipulate objects at a level roughly equivalent to human beings were making their way from research labs into the marketplace. These robots could not "think" creatively like human beings, but that did not matter. Massive AI systems evolved rapidly and allowed machines to perform in ways that seemed very human.

Humanoid robots soon cost less than the average car, and prices kept falling. A typical model had two arms, two legs and the normal human-type sensors like vision, hearing and touch. Power came from small, easily recharged fuel cells. The humanoid form was preferred, as opposed to something odd like R2-D2, because a humanoid shape fit easily into an environment designed around the human body. A humanoid robot could ride an escalator, climb stairs, drive a car, and so on without any trouble.

Once the humanoid robot became a commodity item, robots began to move in and replace humans in the workplace in a significant way. The first wave of replacement began around 2030, starting with jobs in the fast food industry. Robots also filled janitorial and housekeeping positions in hotels, motels, malls, airports, amusement parks and so on.

The economics of one of these humanoid robots made the decision to buy them almost automatic. In 2030 you could buy a humanoid robot for about $10,000. That robot could clean bathrooms, take out trash, wipe down tables, mop floors, sweep parking lots, mow grass and so on. One robot replaced three six-hour-a-day employees. The owner fired the three employees and in just four months the owner re-covered the cost of the robot. The robot would last for many years and would happily work 24 hours a day. The robot also did a far better job—for example, the bathrooms were absolutely spotless. It was impossible to pass up a deal like that, so corporations began buying armies of humanoid robots to replace human employees.

The first completely robotic fast food restaurant opened in 2031. It had some rough edges, but by 2035 the rough edges were gone and by 2040 most restaurants were completely robotic. By 2055 the robots were everywhere. The changeover was that fast. It was a startling, amazing trans-formation and the whole thing happened in only 25 years or so starting in 2030.

In 2055 the nation hit a big milestone—over half of the American workforce was unemployed, and the number was still rising. Nearly every "normal" job that had been filled by a human being in 2001 was filled by a robot instead. At restaurants, robots did all the cooking, cleaning and order taking. At construction sites, robots did everything—Robots poured the concrete, laid brick, built the home's frame, put in the windows and doors, sided the house, roofed it, plumbed it, wired it, hung the drywall, painted it, etc. At the airport, robots flew the planes, sold the tickets, moved the luggage, handled security, kept the building clean and managed air traffic control. At the hospital robots cared for the patients, cooked and delivered the food, cleaned every-thing and handled many of the administrative tasks. At the mall, stores were stocked, cleaned and clerked by robots. At the amusement park, hundreds of robots ran the rides, cleaned the park and sold the concessions. On the roads, robots drove all the cars and trucks. Companies like Fedex, UPS and the post office had huge numbers of robots instead of people sorting packages, driving trucks and making deliveries.

By 2055 robots had taken over the workplace and there was no turning back.

The Inevitable Transformation

I know what you are thinking. You are thinking, "This is *impossible*—there will not be humanoid robots in 2055. It is a ridiculous suggestion." But they will be here. Humanoid robots are as inevitable as airplanes. . . .

There were millions of people in 1900 who believed that humans would never fly. They were completely wrong. However, I don't think *anyone* in 1900 could imagine the B-52 happening in 54 years.

Over the next 55 years, the same thing will happen to us with robots. In the process, the entire employment landscape in America will change.

> "Developing new machines simply isn't worth it; better just to hire a bunch of actual humans."

Robots Are Not Replacing People

Doug Saunders

In the following viewpoint, Doug Saunders dismisses predictions that robots will eventually make human labor unnecessary. Instead, Saunders argues that cheap human workers—especially immigrant laborers—are becoming more attractive to cost-conscious industries. As a result, Saunders says, businesses are decreasing investments in expensive machines and employing large numbers of low-wage workers to fill factories, customer service centers, and other labor-intensive jobs. Doug Saunders is a columnist for the Globe and Mail, *a national Canadian newspaper.*

As you read, consider the following questions:

1. What three factors does Saunders say have made human labor so cheap in the modern age?

Doug Saunders, "Why You Don't Have a Robot Maid," *Globe and Mail* (Toronto, Canada), February 11, 2006, p. F3. Copyright © 2006 Globe Interactive, a division of Bell Globemedia Publishing, Inc. Reproduced by permission.

2. According to the author, why did the telecommunications industry abandon its research into voice-recognition machines to perform customer service tasks?

3. In his nineteen-year study of American agriculture, as cited by Saunders, what did Philip Martin conclude about the industry's trends in labor-saving capital investment?

The newspaper was dated May 29, 1905, and its front-page headline, rude as it was, seemed a distillation of the era to come: "The Machine: Will It Replace the China-Man? Many New Contrivances Just as Cheap, Dependable. . . . Industrious Race May Soon Be Bereft of Purpose."

Of course, it's too true to be real. The satire of a historic paper, created by the talented editors of the mock-newspaper *The Onion*, captures the era perfectly—both the piquant racial attitudes of the time and, more importantly, the overarching theme that would dominate the century to come.

"Machines replace workers" could be the one-sentence synopsis of the 20th century, a message that ricocheted through political movements and popular culture.

From *Modern Times* to *How Green Was My Valley* to *Roger and Me*, from the time-and-motion man to the robotic arm, we learned to think of economic progress in terms of increasingly cheap and powerful equipment doing away with the jobs, and livelihoods, of increasingly dispensable human labourers. Entire categories of people were rendered nonexistent—stevedores, riveters, stenographers, icemen, typesetters, filing clerks.

In the works of [director] Fritz Lang or [science-fiction author] Isaac Asimov, we imagined a future where humans served little purpose beyond the consumption of machine-made goods.

Workers Replace Machines

We are so consumed by this 20th-century narrative that we seem unable to notice that something entirely different is now happening to the world. In the past few years, I've been noticing a new storyline dominating the economy around me: Workers replace machines.

In dozens of industries around the world, employers are discovering that people have become so cheap—thanks to low-cost air travel, relatively liberal immigration, and open economies—that developing new machines simply isn't worth it; better just to hire a bunch of actual humans.

This could become the theme of our age. It also comes as a major surprise: A decade ago, we expected the information-technology revolution to bring about the final End of Work. If even the educated, "symbolic manipulator" jobs could now be done by machines, what use would there be for employment?

Yet what has happened is quite the opposite. The, uh, China-Man (well, to be accurate, the woman and man from China, India, Poland, Turkey, northern Africa, Central and South America and a dozen other places) is doing away with the New Contrivance.

Here in Europe, this is strikingly visible. In many countries, farms have stopped investing in new equipment, instead letting machines rust and using low-wage labour. Like U.S farms did in the 1980s, African and European farms are replacing machines with people.

If you watch a house being built in England these days, the site seems much more crowded—and less high-tech—than it did a generation ago: The Poles who do the jobs are more skilled and less expensive than the Irish workers were back then, so the construction industry has actually de-technologized.

The outstanding example of this trend is the Indian call centre. Until the late 1990s, huge sums were being spent on

Robots Perform a Variety of Tasks

The number of robots in the world today is approaching 1,000,000, with almost half that number in Japan and just 15% in the US. A couple of decades ago, 90% of robots were used in car manufacturing, typically on assembly lines doing a variety of repetitive tasks. Today only 50% are in automobile plants, with the other half spread out among other factories, laboratories, warehouses, energy plants, hospitals, and many other industries.

Robots are used for assembling products, handling dangerous materials, spray-painting, cutting and polishing, inspection of products. The number of robots used in tasks as diverse as cleaning sewers, detecting bombs and performing intricate surgery is increasing steadily, and will continue to grow in coming years.

Jim Pinto, www.automation.com.

research into increasingly advanced voice-recognition machines to answer our phone calls and deal with our orders, inquiries and complaints.

While the latest computer technology is capable of perfecting these synthetic versions of Ernestine the Operator, this line of research has been all but abandoned. Why spend money developing a synthetic telephone personality, when the real thing can be had, in Bangalore, for a much lower price?

More Immigrants, Fewer Machines

To witness this revolution, you might need to look no further than your own house. I'm reminded of a terrific history of *Mary Poppins* by Caitlin Flanagan in a recent issue of *The New Yorker*. Each time the movie was re-released, in 1964, 1973 and 1980, she writes, it was seen by children who grew up in a culture where "nannies were as unfamiliar to middle-class neighbourhoods as Jaguars and Martians."

But those children (children like me) grew up to hire their own servants—cleaning ladies, nannies, people to do the gardening. "Nannies have become a force in American life," she writes, "because of the three-decade-long influx of middle-class mothers to the work force, and the more recent wave of cheap female immigrant labour."

Economists have noticed this. Philip Martin at the University of California has become something of an expert on the advent of capital-saving labour. His studies showed the great U.S. immigration boom of the 1980s and early 1990s caused his country's farming industry to do away with harvesting technology: During the 19-year period of relatively open immigration beginning in 1980, he found, investment in labour-saving technology dropped by 46.7 per cent.

"All economists would agree that necessity is the mother of invention, and that more workers takes the pressure off of employers to find labour-saving alternatives," he told me. "The shorthand expression for this is that both Japanese and German auto makers asked for migrants in the late 1960s, and the Japanese [who didn't get immigrants] got robots, while Germany got Turks."

Both industries did very well, and both countries enjoyed full employment. Now, both countries are facing a dilemma: Whether to lower their wages or to export their industry (many Volkswagens are now made in low-wage Poland).

Immigrants Are the Robots of the Modern Age

But this isn't the same old story. People like Mr. Martin oppose immigration because they believe it lowers productivity (it discourages companies from investing in equipment). But that belief really applies only to agriculture, where the workers are illiterate and unskilled.

Today's migrant workers are often highly educated and literate. Everyone who has cleaned my house or cared for my children—dozens of people over the past decade—has had more education than me. And those call-centre workers are hired for their literacy.

This week, the European Commission produced a fascinating study of the effects of two years of wide-open borders across both the rich and the poor halves of the continent. Yes, it noted, Eastern Europeans have flooded the economies of some countries. Those countries, such as Ireland, happen to have both the lowest unemployment rates and the highest productivity rates in the world. They have not displaced any existing jobs; rather, their availability has created entirely new sectors of economic activity.

But behind all the data was a shocking realization. These educated, literate, talented people, willing to travel huge distances to create a better life for their children, are the robot arms of our age. They are the worker who has replaced the machine.

Periodical Bibliography

The following articles have been selected to supplement the diverse views presented in this chapter.

Michelle Conlin	"The Easiest Commute of All: The Ranks of Remote Workers Are Swelling as Companies See the Sense in Freeing Them," *Business Week*, December 12, 2005.
James Fallows	"A Thousand Words: Cameras and Telephones Coming Together—and Bringing People Together—in Ways That Can Shape Society," *Atlantic Monthly*, April 2006.
Mary Kathleen Flynn	"Pull the Plug on Tech Distractions," *U.S. News & World Report*, December 26, 2005.
Leo Lewis	"The Robots Are Coming, So Get Ready to Order Your Drinks . . . ," *Times* (London), December 3, 2005.
Daniel Memmi	"The Nature of Virtual Communities," *AI & Society*, June 2006.
Heather Menzies	"No Life in the Fast Lane: Rediscovering Slow Can Liberate Us from the Tyranny of 24/7," *United Church Observer*, November 2005.
Anna Quindlen	"The Face in the Crowd: Looking Someone Straight in the Eye Is an Age-Old Incentive to Do the Right Thing, but There's Precious Little of It in the Computer Age," *Newsweek*, March 20, 2006.
Dave Rensberger	"Gadget Glut: A Tale of Convergence Suffocation," *Searcher*, June 2006.
Kathleen Richardson	"Mechanical People: Will Robots Ever Serve as Substitutes for Human Companions?" *New Scientist*, June 24, 2006.
Brad Stone	"Not Human Enough: As Japan's Robot Experiment Shows, Creating a Lifelike Android Is Beyond the Reach of Science," *Newsweek International*, September 4, 2006.

OPPOSING
VIEWPOINTS®
SERIES

CHAPTER 2

What Impact Does Technology Have on Education?

Chapter Preface

In 2005, the Kaiser Foundation reported that children between the ages of eight and eighteen were packing more media exposure into the quarter of the day that they routinely spent with electronic media (including television, computers, compact disc players, and cell phones). In order to pack in more media, today's children are juggling multiple media at one time. That is, they are watching television while downloading music from the Internet while talking to friends on the phone. The Kaiser Foundation found this trend in multitasking was unique to the modern media-saturated era and dubbed the children of this new age Generation M.

Some observers of Generation M believe this new breed of children, born into a world that is comfortable with computers and the Internet, is exceptional for its ability to handle and manipulate technology. With some older generations still anxious about technology and often confounded by each innovation, the new generation seems not only fluent in the use of new technologies but also eager to master the latest application. And they seem to multitask quite well, effortlessly shifting from one medium to another. Patricia Greenfield, director of the Children's Digital Media Center at the University of California, Los Angeles, agrees. In a comment to *Newsweek*, she noted, "Kids are getting better at paying attention to several things at once." However, Greenfield was quick to add, "But there is a cost in that you don't go into any one thing in as much depth."

David E. Meyer, the director of the Brain, Cognition and Action Laboratory at the University of Michigan, supports Greenfield's view. He believes that the mystique of Generation M is misunderstood. The brain cannot, he asserts, multitask; instead it parcels its attention to select tasks over time. In this respect, a person may seem to be able to handle several tasks at once, but he or she is really only moving from one to another, usually giving less than full attention to each. Meyer told *Time*, "If a teenager is trying to have a conversation on an e-mail chat line while doing algebra, she'll suffer a decrease in efficiency, compared to if she just thought about algebra until she was done. People may think otherwise, but it's a myth. With such complicated tasks [you] will never, ever be able to overcome the inherent limitations in the brain for processing information during multitasking."

In the following chapter, critics and commentators debate how technology is shaping the education of Generation M. Some believe that engaging the generation's proclivity for technology and multimedia gadgetry will stimulate learning and keep children interested in education. Others fear that computers, the Internet, and other additions to the modern classroom are handicapping traditional teaching methods and occupying too much of children's time in school and at home.

> *"Computer-enabled students spend more time preening their reports than understanding the subject matter."*

Technology Is Hurting Education

Clifford Stoll

In the following viewpoint, Clifford Stoll argues that computer education in the classroom hurts students and the learning environment. He claims that computers encourage students to waste time and do not teach them the basics of problem solving or the principles of liberal arts. Stoll asserts that computer literacy in the classroom translates into prettier reports and graphics-rich projects but does not enhance the understanding of curricula subjects. Clifford Stoll is an astronomer, computer systems administrator, and the author of High Tech Heretic: Why Computers Don't Belong in the Classroom and Other Reflections by a Computer Contrarian.

As you read, consider the following questions:

1. In Stoll's view, what kinds of computer tasks do students need to know to function in a learning environment?

Clifford Stoll, "Pull the Plug! Computers in the Classroom Don't Solve Any Problems—in Fact, They Often Make Things Worse," *CIO* Magazine, September 1, 2000.

2. How does Stoll counter the argument that schools need to bring computers into the classroom because computers are ubiquitous in society and business?

3. What parts of school curricula are disappearing to make way for computers and computer labs, according to Stoll?

Among the challenges confronting our elementary and high school students today, one might list short attention spans, lack of discipline, cynical attitudes, too much television, low regard for teachers or little interest in reading. OK: Which of these problems are solved by a classroom computer? Which, on the other hand, are made worse?

The one thing that the networked computer does well is to give our kids more information, faster. But lack of information simply isn't a problem in any school I've visited. Indeed, most teachers complain that they haven't enough time to teach the information that's already available.

Some might argue that the goal of wiring schools is to replace outdated textbooks with the latest information from the Net. But most subjects don't change that quickly. The core of physics and chemistry, for example, evolves slowly. Schools certainly don't need the Internet to teach poetry or literature. And only a fool would teach current events from a textbook— that's the purpose of magazines, newspapers and the daily news.

Little Need for Computer Literacy at School

Maybe we're wiring our classrooms to promote computer literacy. But how much computing does a student need to be taught? I'd say that a high school graduate oughta be able to use a word processor, manipulate a spreadsheet, know what a database does, use e-mail, browse the Web and use a search engine. OK, how long did it take you to learn to use a word processor? A day? Maybe three? Did it take you a week to figure out how to surf the Web? Aside from the mechanical typing lessons, this just isn't challenging stuff. And whatever the problems confronting our students, fear of computers isn't one of 'em. Nor is the inability to use the Internet. Quite the opposite: Kids quickly take to computers and will happily spend hours sending e-mail, logging into chat rooms and generally fooling around online.

Computer literacy doesn't demand the same level of instruction as English, American history or physics. Spending semesters teaching computing simply subtracts time from other subjects. It's one more way to dumb down the school, giving the appearance of teaching futuristic subjects while dodging the important topics. You can learn how to use computers anytime in life, but some subjects really are best learned when you're young—foreign languages, musical instruments, just to name two.

The fact is, computers don't belong in the classroom. Not only do they not help solve any educational problems, but they very often make existing problems worse.

All Flash, No Substance

Whenever I point out the dubious value of computers in schools, I hear the comment, "Look, computers are everywhere, so we have to bring them into the classroom." Well, automobiles are everywhere too. They play a damned important part in our society, and it's hard to get a job if you can't drive. But we don't teach "automobile literacy." Nor do we make cars a central part of the curriculum—indeed, many schools are now dropping driver's ed, recognizing that teenagers can learn to drive without intensive schooling.

And yes, computers seem ubiquitous, but that's no reason to bring them into the classroom. Television is certainly omnipresent, but it's been relegated to a fairly minor role in schools. I don't hear politicians worrying about some "television divide" separating those with the tube from those without.

Computers Distract from Learning

In bucking the [computers in the classroom] trend, the Toronto Waldorf School is arguably doing its students a favour. While computers clearly have a place in education (Waldorf introduces them in Grade 9), the evidence is mounting that our obsessive use of information technology is dumbing us down, adults as well as kids. While they can be engaging and resourceful tools for learning—if used in moderation—computers and the Internet can also distract kids from homework, encourage superficial and uncritical thinking, replace face-to-face interaction between students and teachers, and lead to compulsive behaviour.

At least some teens recognize the problem. Fifteen-year-old Colin Johnson of Toronto sits down at his computer at 4 most afternoons. He whizzes through his homework in half an hour, and then starts surfing, gaming and chatting with friends on MSN until 1 a.m., when he goes to bed. The tenth-grader is failing science, but otherwise getting by. "I procrastinate a lot more than before," he says, acknowledging that "everybody's marks suffer to some degree" if they spend as much time as he does online.

Sue Ferguson, Maclean's, *June 6, 2005.*

Computers encourage students to turn in visually exciting hypermedia projects, often at the expense of written compositions and hand-drawn projects. Pasting a fancy graphic into a science report doesn't mean an eighth grader has learned anything. Nor does a downloaded report from the Internet suggest that a student has any understanding of the material.

Instead, the emphasis on professional reports sends students the message that appearance and fonts are more important than content. Indeed, for most schoolwork, searching online source materials not only isn't necessary, it's often counterproductive. Computer-enabled students spend more time preening their reports than understanding the subject matter.

What Is Lost to Make Room for Computers

By wiring our schools we make a funding decision about what's academically important. Next time a principal or school-board member shows off a modern computer lab, ask 'em this: "What was in this room before these computers?"

I asked that question recently and got the following answers:

- "We converted the library into the computer lab. With the multimedia encyclopedias, we no longer need as many books."
- "Oh, we used to teach art in this room."
- "This used to be our machine shop."
- "A music studio. . . ."

And if you think technology cuts into only school libraries and music programs, you should check out high school chemistry labs. The days of test tubes and Bunsen burners are disappearing fast as school districts get scared of students handling chemicals. Too easy to spill acid, burn a finger or build a bomb. As safety concerns drive up the cost of real labs, schools turn to high-tech solutions: computer simulations. Like learning to drive a simulated car, it's fun, but it sure ain't the real thing.

Politicians tell us to wire our schools so that graduates will be prepared for jobs. But by focusing on computers, plenty of technical jobs are being bypassed: High schools are slyly dropping courses in plumbing, auto mechanics, carpentry and cooking. Do we really expect a future without pipes, cars and restaurants?

Shouldn't computers reduce school costs by making administrative activities more efficient? I wish it were so. As computers become widely adopted in elementary and high schools, they add a whole new layer of school administrators and middle managers. These include content administrators to watch over what the students view and technology specialists to show teachers how best to use the digital machines.

Wasting Teachers' Time

And don't forget that school computers need technical support—it's silly to expect English teachers to install and maintain the high school's file servers. In business, you figure one full-time support person for every 20 or 30 workstations. The tech folk aren't cheap, and they don't teach. Each program—even the simplest—requires someone to get the computers ready. Inevitably, it's the teacher. The dirty secret of educational technology is that computers waste teachers' time.

Around the country, communities float 30-year bond issues to buy computers that will be obsolete within five years. Wiring a school typically costs thousands of dollars per classroom, and evolving communications systems will mean that the work will have to be redone within a decade. Classroom software has a surprisingly short life as the curriculum, computer and educational climates change. Educational technology saves money? Nah.

A Nation of Dolts

In short, no amount of Web searching can make up for a lack of critical thinking or communication skills. No microprocessor can replace the creative interplay of hand, clay and art teacher. No online astronomy program can engender the same sense of awe as first seeing the rings of Saturn through a telescope. No computer will encourage a budding athlete to run faster, kick harder or jump higher. With or without a computer, a mediocre instructor will never kindle a love for learning. And a good teacher doesn't need the Internet to inspire her students to excellence.

Want a nation of dolts? Center the curriculum around technology—teach with videos, computers and multimedia systems. Aim for the highest possible scores on standardized tests. Push aside such less vocationally applicable subjects as music, art and history. No doubt about it: Dolts are what we'll get.

| "It is critical for teachers to ... adapt information technology to the methods and content of their instruction."

Technology Needs to Be Emphasized in Education

Mortimer B. Zuckerman

Mortimer B. Zuckerman is the chairman and editor in chief of U.S. News & World Report *and is the publisher of the New York* Daily News. *In the following viewpoint, he argues that computers belong in the classroom. According to Zuckerman, computer-aided learning is interactive and can bring the world and its wonders to every student. Furthermore, the potential reaches beyond the traditional classroom setting, Zuckerman states, as distance learning and tutoring can empower students both at home and in school.*

As you read, consider the following questions:

1. Why does Zuckerman believe that computers should be moved out of special labs and brought directly into the classroom setting?

2. In the author's opinion, how can parents benefit from their children's immersion in online learning?

3. As Zuckerman reports, how did computer learning impact the West Virginia schools during the experiment launched in 1990?

Students of almost every age are far ahead of their teachers in computer literacy. This is especially true of younger kids with younger parents. So how is this digital revolution affecting education? A binary answer: Not enough. According to a federal study, most schools are essentially unchanged today despite reforms and increased investment in computers.

The general pattern is for computers to be in a computer lab—something separate and apart like a Bunsen burner. Why? Students who have mastered the wonders of the Internet at home know that with a desktop computer they can do everything faster—take and save notes, write and do research. With guidance, kids can learn these skills at home, especially when high-quality interactive programming becomes more widely available in science, history, math, geography, and languages. There is much work to be done in creating these electronic assets, however. And it is critical for teachers to join the revolution—to adapt information technology to the methods and content of their instruction.

Overcoming the Bounds of Time and Space

Goodbye, Mr. Chips—hello, Mr. Chip!

What does this mean? It means a teacher can take the class around the world electronically to look at the development of civilizations in Egypt, Greece, Rome, Latin America. A Spanish class in Idaho can talk to students in Bilbao. It means linking biology students in Chicago with a researcher at a microscope in San Francisco, history students with a curator at the National Portrait Gallery, technology students with the National Air and Space Museum in Washington. Just think, teachers using digitized collections of Civil War photographs and oral histories can immerse students in original building blocks of

American history. Students can take virtual trips and collaborate with other students around the world and research in the best libraries in the country. Teachers can compare techniques with colleagues around the country and create teaching modules on everything from calculus to cloning. Distance learning can explode the number of courses a student might take online with peers, retired experts, and master teachers and writers. Observations can be posted on the Web for use by thousands of other teachers and students. Even the smallest one-room schoolhouse in the wilds can tap into great teaching on an infinite variety of subjects.

There is no limit to the possibilities. Distance learning can include Advanced Placement courses and special tutoring for the learning disabled whose talents are not developed in regular classes. With electronic links, textbooks will morph into digital versions with interactive sections, videoconferencing, and dramatic television sequences. What excitement! And all this can be kept as fresh as milk. In the language of [technology prophet and social critic] Marshall McLuhan, video is a "cool medium"; that is to say, it lends itself to high audience participation. Parents can also benefit by viewing their children's work online, exchanging E-mails with teachers, and watching webcasts from distance schooling. This is the 21st-century version of distance learning. What it offers is much more flexibility in time, place, and pace of instruction, an opportunity to create a superb instructional environment adapted to each school's particular needs.

Reaping the Benefits

Of course, teachers and school boards need to be convinced that the Internet can make their schools more effective. Look at West Virginia. In 1990, it launched a statewide effort to use technology to improve its struggling schools. Computers were gradually integrated into classes, beginning with the earliest grades, while the teachers received extensive training over seven years. The result? West Virginia jumped to 11th from 33rd on national achievement tests.

To extend state-of-the-art approaches to every school in our new technological universe we also must deal with cost. Even though laptop prices are plunging, schools are going to have to develop innovative budgeting at both state and local levels to acquire the funds for technology, training, and programming.

We are on the threshold of the most radical change in American education in over a century as schools leave the industrial age to join the information age. For most of the past century, our schools were designed to prepare children for jobs on factory lines. Kids lived by the bell, moved through schools as if on conveyor belts, and learned to follow instructions. But today many of these factories are overseas, leaving behind a factory-based school system for an information age.

[The Soviet satellite] Sputnik once woke up America's leaders to how far we had fallen behind the Soviet Union.

This generation's Sputnik moment arrived with the economic competition of high skills and low wages from Asia and academic performances far surpassing our own.

Here with the Web is the way for America to use the marvels it created to end the regression in our competitive and academic performance. Let's get to it.

> *"The disparity in technology access must be viewed as a national threat—to our economic competitiveness, our civil rights, and our national creed of equal opportunity."*

There Is a Digital Divide

Andy Carvin

In the following viewpoint, Andy Carvin claims that though the issue has virtually disappeared from media attention, the "digital divide" still exists. The digital divide—the term coined to describe the disparity between those who have access to computers and the Internet and those who do not—is still drawn along racial lines, Carvin says. He contends that fewer African American and Hispanic students have computers in schools or at home, and that this lack will eventually handicap America economically as other countries focus on teaching computer literacy to legions of their young people. Andy Carvin is the coordinator of the Digital Divide Network, an online community for educators and policy makers concerned with bridging the digital divide.

Andy Carvin, "The Gap: Once a Hot Topic, the Digital Divide Seems All But Forgotten, While the Poor, Mainly Black and Hispanic, Are Still Being Left Behind," *School Library Journal*, vol. 52, no. 3, March 2006, pp. 70–72. Copyright © 2006 Reed Business Information, Inc. Reproduced from *School Library Journal*, a Cahners/R. R. Bowker publication, by permission.

As you read, consider the following questions:

1. As Carvin reports, why does Reina Huerta say many teachers in "challenging environments" are ill equipped to provide technology instruction to their students?

2. Of the four ethnic groups mentioned in the author's viewpoint, which was least likely to have Internet access at home, according to the 2004 federal study "A Nation Online"?

3. What does Carvin say many foreign governments have created in order to improve technological education?

This year, 2006, marks the 10th anniversary of the advent of the digital divide—a major societal challenge that, sadly, has been pushed aside and forgotten in recent years.

Rewind to 1996: middle-class Americans were just beginning to explore the possibilities of the Internet as a tool for education, civic engagement, and entertainment. Yet less affluent citizens, lacking the necessary skills and exposure, did not enjoy the same access to these opportunities.

The so-called "Digital Divide" made prominent headlines that year when high-profile pundits, from President Bill Clinton to network news anchors, popularized the term in addressing the growing inequities that appeared to accompany the technological revolution. Today, however, you're not likely to hear much mention of the digital divide on the news or your favorite political blog. As with other political and social issues, conversation about the digital divide ebbs and flows—and for several years now we've been wallowing at a low watermark.

A Struggle to Get Computers into the Right Hands

Just what happened to the digital divide debate? With the proliferation of the Internet and so many people online today, you might assume that the problem has dissipated. But the reality is far more complex than that.

Just ask Reina Huerta, the technology integration specialist at the Tito Puente Educational Complex in New York's East Harlem. A 23-year teaching veteran of the New York City public schools who's also served there as a certified library media specialist, Huerta spends her days putting computers and other technology tools into the hands of teachers and staff. It's a struggle, she says, especially in a challenging environment, where teachers are often overwhelmed by more pressing issues like class management, behavior problems, and transient students. Many staff also come out of the local neighborhood, says Huerta, and so haven't had the means to gain the same familiarity with computers that's pretty much a given among middle-class workers.

While the demographics of East Harlem have shifted slightly over the years—more Spanish-speaking immigrants these days come from Mexico [instead of from the Caribbean]—it remains a poor, struggling community. At Tito Puente—which serves more than 800 sixth through eighth graders, plus a special needs program—over 90 percent of the primarily Hispanic and African-American students qualify for free lunch.

So mention the digital divide to Huerta, who splits her job between Tito Puente and a similarly underserved elementary school in the Bronx, and she responds, almost in a whisper, "Oh, yes, it's still there."

The National Picture

Indeed, the latest national figures indicate the persistence of a disturbing gap along racial lines. According to "A Nation Online," the last major federal study on the subject published in 2004, Caucasian and Asian-American households were more likely to be online than African-American households, which in turn were more likely to be wired than Latino households. And while overall Web use rose for each demographic group—about 60 percent of U.S. households were online, up from less

The Internet Have-Nots

	Non-Internet Users (Percent)	
	Sept. 2001	**Oct. 2003**
Total Population	44.9	41.3
Gender		
Male	44.8	41.8
Female	45.0	40.8
Race/Ethnicity		
White	38.7	34.9
White Alone	n/a	34.9
Black	58.9	54.4
Black Alone	n/a	54.8
Asian Amer. & Pac. Isl.	37.5	36.9
Asian Amer. & Pac. Isl. Alone	n/a	37.0
Hispanic (of any race)	66.6	62.8
Employment Status		
Employed	33.4	29.3
Not Employed	62.0	57.2
Family Income		
Less than $15,000	74.1	68.8
$15,000–$24,999	65.6	62.0
$25,000–$34,999	54.7	51.1
$35,000–$49,999	41.7	37.9
$50,000–$74,999	31.1	28.2
$75,000 & above	19.6	17.1
$75,000–$99,999	n/a	20.2
$100,000–$149,999	n/a	14.9
$150,000 & above	n/a	13.9
Educational Attainment		
Less Than High School	86.3	84.5
High School Diploma/GED	58.9	55.5
Some College	36.5	31.4
Bachelor's Degree	17.8	15.1
Beyond Bachelor's Degree	15.0	12.0
Location of the Person's Household		
Rural	45.9	42.8
Urban	44.5	40.8
Urban Not Central City	41.2	37.5
Urban Central City	49.7	46.0

TAKEN FROM: U.S. Bureau of Census, Current Population Survey supplements, September 2001, and October 2003.

than 20 percent in 1997—the hierarchy of access has remained essentially the same for the last decade.

Of the income divide, the report revealed that more than 80 percent of households earning more than $70,000 per year are online, compared to barely 30 percent of households earning less than $15,000 a year.

For me, though, the most telling statistics relate to education. Nearly nine out of 10 households in which someone has attained graduate-level education were online. In contrast, less than one in five households, 16 percent of people without a high school diploma, had Internet access. Though shocking, these statistics should come as no surprise. Despite all the incredible advances in streaming video and Web-based multimedia, the Internet remains a text-dominant medium. If you lack a strong foundation in literacy skills, all the Internet access in the world isn't going to do you a lot of good.

The Need to Invest in Tech Education

Unfortunately, the digital divide is rarely addressed as a major policy issue in America. But as the U.S. struggles to improve its schools, while dragging its heels at improving our national broadband infrastructure, countries like India and China are churning out highly skilled young people for their workforces. At the same time, Nordic countries and Korea deploy ubiquitous Internet access. Other nations are creating government ministries to spur technological and educational innovation, while American digital divide policies have fallen off the docket. America is losing its competitiveness because we're not making the necessary investments in education and infrastructure.

Fortunately, there is still positive work being done. The federal e-rate program continues to enable low-income schools and libraries to connect to the Internet, while nonprofit and private sector entities invest in local and national efforts dedicated to bridging the gap. Meanwhile, copyright initiatives like

Creative Commons ease the way for people to publish their own content for broad public use. And open courseware initiatives from universities, such as MIT [Massachusetts Institute of Technology], are making some of the most coveted curriculum freely available, whether you can afford to attend the brick-and-mortar institutions or not.

The challenge remains, however, to get the digital divide back on the national agenda. The disparity in technology access must be viewed as a national threat—to our economic competitiveness, our civil rights, and our national creed of equal opportunity. While it may be true that seven out of 10 Americans are online, we shouldn't pat ourselves on the back just yet. Not as long as disenfranchised, underserved Americans remain on the wrong side of the divide.

"There is no such thing as the digital divide."

There Is No Digital Divide

Ejovi Nuwere

Ejovi Nuwere argues in the following viewpoint that the "digital divide" is a misnamed crisis. He states that the discrepancy between those who have access to technology and those who do not has nothing to do with the technology itself. The underlying problem, he insists, is the financial disparity between rich and poor, and this factor cannot be remedied by simply providing more computer and Internet service to the have-nots. Ejovi Nuwere is a computer security professional and an author who grew up in an impoverished borough of New York City.

As you read, consider the following questions:

1. In Nuwere's view, what do the poor lack when it comes to technology or any other interest enjoyed by the wealthy?

2. Why has the term "digital divide" made the issue more difficult to address, according to the author?

3. Instead of handing out computers to impoverished areas, what does Nuwere believe companies and governments should do to bridge the gap between rich and poor?

There is no such thing as the digital divide. I hear the term used all the time, but it has this vague elusive definition that just doesn't sit well with me. It's often used to define the gap in technical knowledge and usage between the middle-upper-class America and poorer, often minority, America. On one hand, it has also been used to define one of the evils that have come of our embrace of technology while on the other hand some argue that using technology could help bridge that gap.

These views are not only wrong, they are dangerous. If there is a digital divide then there is also a banking and investing divide, an expensive pets and watches divide and an aviation hobbyist divide. There are of course huge gaps in the subjects fore-mentioned but they are not gaps created or fueled by the subjects themselves. The gap is much like the gap in technology between the haves and have not, a financial one.

The Wrong Approach

In general the poor tend to have a lack of understanding when it comes to investing and find aviation as a hobby financially unfeasible, and the same applies to technology. We all know that giving planes and large bank accounts to the poor won't solve these problems. Yet that is how we are attacking the gap in technology: giving away computers in poor neighborhoods and wiring schools with high-speed Internet access as a bandage and then walking away.

The use of the term "digital divide" has convinced many people that technology is the solution to what is actually an economic problem. But it is not. Technology is a great tool in helping to bridge the economic divide, but it alone cannot

No Easy Fix for the Digital Divide

The digital divide is not a problem in itself, but a symptom of deeper, more important divides: of income, development and literacy. Fewer people in poor countries than in rich ones own computers and have access to the internet simply because they are too poor, are illiterate, or have other more pressing concerns, such as food, health care and security. So even if it were possible to wave a magic wand and cause a computer to appear in every household on earth, it would not achieve very much: a computer is not useful if you have no food or electricity and cannot read.

Economist, *March 10, 2005.*

solve our problems. Placing computers into schools is only the first step; modifying the education system to integrate new technology into the learning process is the next.

Some would have us place thousands of computers in poor rural countries and connect them to wireless networks to promote commerce, but these measures will only take us so far. In many developing countries road infrastructure and transportation infrastructure are non-existent. All the online orders in the world wouldn't be able to help them unless investments are made to develop physical infrastructure.

Solution Has Nothing to Do with Computers

Let's not make technology a cop-out. It is cheaper for companies and governments to spend $10,000 on computers than to really invest the millions needed to promote business development and infrastructure building in poor rural areas. Cheaper than looking at the problem of why we have such a large economic gap between the rich and the poor.

The use of the term "digital divide" only fuels such ill responsibility. . . . Let's leave behind bad habits. Ask yourself what is the cause of our technology divide? Once you find the answer, I believe you will agree with me that whatever the solution is it has little to do with computers.

> *"Tech-savvy kids are adept at managing large amounts of data with technology . . . [and] teaching themselves how to solve problems in an interactive environment."*

Children Are Technologically Skilled

Susan Smith Nash

In the following viewpoint, Susan Smith Nash argues that children of the Information Age are technologically gifted. This interaction with technology and vast amounts of data has made young people adept at manipulating and managing information. In addition, being part of new communications networks has aided children in developing useful learning and research skills. Susan Smith Nash is a contributing writer for XplanaZine, a Web-based magazine, and the associate dean of liberal arts at Excelsior College in Albany, New York.

As you read, consider the following questions:

1. What instructional benefits do modern video games have, according to Nash?

Susan Smith Nash, "Has Technology Made Kids Smarter? Education and the Tech-Savvy Child," *XplanaZine* (Online Learning), June 2, 2006. www.xplanazine.com. Reproduced by permission of the author.

2. In the author's view, what do tech-savvy children do with information that is not immediately relevant to their lives?

3. What failures does Nash attribute to the Baby Boomer generation that are not shared by their modern, tech-savvy children?

I had an interesting conversation with my son about e-learning and social networking. He described the way the Internet makes one think and behave differently than in times past.

"We're smarter than your generation, Mom," he said. "We've moved beyond that. We evolved."

Could he be right? It occurs to me that Boomer and Gen-X parents do not quite realize that the Internet, watching media (including films and television), and playing video games are not the same passive activities that they were during *Leave It to Beaver, Pong* or Colecovision days. Video games can be massively multi-player, so playing them requires a great deal of skill, and communication ability. When they download and edit movies and music, play games, and communicate with friends, tech-savvy kids are problem-solving, recognizing patterns, increasing hand-eye coordination, cataloguing events, determining cause-effect relationships, predicting sequences, and more.

Further, as they download music and film, they develop extreme film and music literacy. Granted, it's not in a form that is easily tested, and the knowledge gained here won't make anyone a *wunderkind* in the local No Child Left Behind test battery. Nevertheless, they do know how to get the information. The trick is to turn it into knowledge, and knowledge that can be used.

Amazing Skills of Tech-Savvy Children

This brings me back to the original question. Are kids today smarter than my generation when we were kids? Part of me agrees, for the following reasons:

Skills Learned in Children's Spare Time

Digital participation is, for the most part, sharpening the minds of Generation M, not dumbing them down.... The skills they're developing are not trivial. They're learning to analyze complex systems with many interacting variables, to master new interfaces, to find and validate information in vast databases, to build and maintain extensive social networks crossing both virtual and real-world environments, to adapt existing technology to new uses. And they're learning all this in their spare time—for fun!

Steven Johnson, Time, *March 27, 2006.*

1. Tech-savvy kids are adept at managing large amounts of data with technology. They are also used to teaching themselves how to solve problems in an interactive environment. As James Paul Gee has described in his book, *What Video Games Have to Teach Us about Teaching and Learning* (2004), when playing a video game, the average child learns quickly how to do effective task analysis in a "real-time" setting and to obtain the necessary information which is available on-demand in order to achieve the goal. This is a perfect example of situated, outcomes-oriented learning, and children of this generation are extremely skilled at it by age 6 or 7, depending on how long they've been playing video games.

2. Today's generation of youth are exposed to vast quantities of information, and they learn to manage, classify, use, and dismiss what is not useful to them. While this is an excellent skill it also may result in distressingly extensive lacunae; that is to say, gigantic gaps in knowledge. If the information is not immediately applicable

and relevant to one's life, it is ignored or dismissed. The positive aspect of this approach is that the average tech-savvy kid will have encyclopedic knowledge in areas that interest him or her. This might include audio files, "cheats" for games, movies on DVD. On the other hand, he or she may know little or nothing about world geography.

3. With the new social networking sites, tech-savvy kids are becoming adept at social development learning, which has been described by [developmental psychologist Lev] Vygotsky and others. According to this theory, people learn through social interaction, and it does not matter whether or not it is face-to-face or virtual. It follows, then, that kids who spend hours instant-messaging or interacting with social networking spaces such as myspace.com, livejournal.com, xanga.com and others, will have experienced an accelerated pace of learning.

4. Comfort with searching and finding information that helps them achieve their objectives in a short period of time is something to marvel at when seeing it in action. Teen-agers are creating web-based businesses of all sorts, and have been extremely effective at generating traffic and revenues. They are also adept at using the internet to solve logistical problems, and they use Mapquest, google-earth, UPS tracking, US Postal service (create your own stamps, etc.) with great success.

5. Image manipulation is not only easy for tech-savvy kids, it is also accompanied by the awareness that each digital image is manipulated, resulting in a worldview that does not necessarily trust appearances.

Comparing Generations

When one considers how kids have been spending their free time with information technology, it is no wonder that they are bored by school. You don't have to be an "Indigo Child" [especially gifted or advanced children] to find a 50-minute traditional class where students sit dutifully in hard chairs behind desks, listening to the teacher, taking notes, then taking tests, to be utterly stultifying. It is enough to convince a parent that homeschool or "unschooling" [self-directed learning philosophy] could actually be better than a structured classroom experience.

Thinking about my son's words, I try to imagine how the current generation of teen-agers might view their Generation X and Baby Boomer parents. The words "narcissistic" and "self-absorbed" occur to me immediately, as I think of the high divorce rates, the "me generation," the "yuppies," and bizarre custody battles in which more concern was given to the family cat and rights to the time-share than to the kids. I do believe that he has a point. Boomer generations can be seen as resisting the notion that everything is always in flux, and that nothing is permanent; thus one can never be smug or complacent. A failure to embrace the notion of constant technological change and upgrades sets up internal resistance to new ideas and structures. I can see how this could lead to a failure to communicate in any meaningful way about process and procedures.

While a great deal of effort is expended in creating online courses and education programs that will appeal to adults, operating under the assumption that the adult learner needs to have the course content presented in a certain way for learning to take place, perhaps it is not too far-fetched to say that the same principles apply to tech-savvy kids.

The specific activities required in the lessons will be different, and the way the material is used will vary. However, the following three learning outcomes can accommodate both generations. Upon successful completion of the course, the student should be able to

1. Make connections between unrelated and/or related items and to support the connections with a rationale based on close analysis of the items;

2. Solve problems using the material and concepts presented in the learning module;

3. Engage in metacognitive tasks and develop skills such as generalization, classification, and abstraction that can transfer from one course to another.

In the meantime, it probably would not be a bad idea to start putting a renewed emphasis on ethics and ethical behavior. After all, this generation and the one after it will be taking care of us one day.

> "[The] erosion of childhood concerns me and computers seem like a river in flood washing away the soil that roots children to the natural world."

Children Need Imaginative Play

David Sobel

David Sobel is the director of Teacher Certification Programs at Antioch New England Graduate School in New Hampshire. He is also the author of four books on children's learning and education. In the following viewpoint, Sobel argues that computers and other technology are being foisted upon children in order to prepare them for life in a technologically sophisticated world. According to Sobel, this goal may seem praiseworthy, but the glut of technology at a young age commonly means a loss of traditional childhood experiences and imaginative play. In Sobel's view, children need to experience the natural world and learn by interacting with it, instead of passively absorbing information from computers and television.

As you read, consider the following questions:

1. According to Sobel, roughly what percentage of children are playing outdoors after school?

2. What skills does the author say "mature" out of children's interaction with concrete materials, caring adults, and managed peer groups?

3. About how many hours of combined television and computer-use time does Sobel think is appropriate for children?

Have you seen the advertisements? The four-year-old sits propped on a couple of pillows gazing into the computer. She is bathed in soft, multi-colored light while the rest of the room is in shadow. The light suggests alpenglow, the radiant magenta softness that high peaks catch from the setting sun while the rest of the landscape is subdued in twilight. The computer glow is supposed to be subtly beautiful; this is a moment of quiet reverence and thoughtful contemplation. The computer industry has discovered a new market—preschool-aged children. . . .

If they can get kids hooked on computers and software at an early age, then manufacturers can be assured of 60 years of techno-consuming. It is just like Louisiana Pacific's practice of planting seedlings to harvest after four decades of growth, and it may be producing the same kind of monotonous monoculture in our children's minds.

A founder of a small school in northern California described his concerns about the computer issue to me. All the parents sending their children to the school had a deep ecological consciousness and were very progressive. But as soon as their children were in first grade they wanted to know, "When is the school going to get computers?" They couldn't really articulate why they thought computers were important for young children, but they were anxious to have their kids jump on the bandwagon so they would not get left behind.

Childhood Takes Time

The pressure on children to be ahead of the curve is accelerating. Yet the timetable for children's neurological development is unchanged. New imaging studies of the developing human brain show that the nervous system matures slowly and that human development is biologically grounded in carefully orchestrated patterns of growth. Healthy neural branching of the developing brain depends on close personal relationships with caring adults and on hands-on experiences in the real world. All of this takes time.

Cognitive development, says psychologist William Crain, "has a certain natural slowness," and individual children have their own optimal pace. The slow pace is marked by behavioral and motivational phases that correspond to biological patterns of growth that are now traceable through scans of the developing human brain. That means the speed of childhood cannot be mechanically calibrated. "Children, like plants, grow according to nature's timetable," writes Crain.

Alliance for Childhood, Tech Tonic:
Towards a New Literacy of Technology, *2004.*

Capitalizing on these latent fears and parental concerns, the advertising hook is, "If you love your child, buy her a computer!" But does the computer really make your preschooler smarter, happier and healthier? Or does it numb her brain and make her just another contributor to the globalization of a consumer-oriented, ecologically destructive culture?

The Lost Joys of Childhood

Regrettably, it is not so clearly black and white. Rather, to paraphrase [singer] Judy Collins, "Something's lost and something's gained in computer use everyday." When children in and out of school are using computers, they are not doing something else. If we understand what they are not doing as well as what they are doing, we will be in a better position to decide what place computers should have in children's lives.

I got a perspective on the after-school situation from talking with an environmental educator who works with a group of fourth graders in Keene, NH, our small city surrounded by parks and woods. This past spring she read the children Alice McLaren's *Roxaboxen*, a book about children creating a fantasy town while growing up in the American West in the 1930's. It is a simple portrait of independent, imaginative play. "Oh, those children are so lucky. I wish we could do that," was the children's response. My friend was surprised. She had assumed the children would easily identify with the children in the story, so she asked them what they did after school. Of the 16 children in the class, two of the children were not allowed to go outside, four said they watched TV or talked on the phone, six went to the recreation center to play video games, and four played outside. If this is a representative sample, then only 25% of nine-year-old children in our safe, all-American city are out playing in the neighborhood after school.

This resonates eerily with a child's comment collected by Richard Louv in research for his book entitled *Childhood's Future*. When Louv asked a group of fourth graders whether they liked to play indoors or outdoors better, one fourth grader responded, "I like to play indoors better 'cause that's where the electrical outlets are." I do not have to tell you what they are playing inside, do I?

This erosion of childhood concerns me and computers seem like a river in flood washing away the soil that roots children to the natural world. Elementary age children, now more than ever, need opportunities to be in their bodies in the world—jumping-rope, bicycling, stream hopping and fort building. It is in this engagement between the limbs of the body and the bones of the earth where true balance and centeredness emerge. . . .

Technology Can Rob Children of Creativity

Like television, computers encourage our children to become couch potatoes. The sophisticated processes of critical thinking, problem-solving and kinesthetic coordination appropriately mature out of children's interaction with concrete materials, caring adults and thoughtfully managed groups of peers. Luring children into the world of pure information and electronic images alienates them from experience and disembodies their learning. But in concert with active learning, computers can enhance the educational experience. In all things, moderation.

I will never forget sitting next to Joseph Chilton Pearce, the noted author of *The Crack in the Cosmic Egg* and *Magical Child*, at a presentation about educational software. *Storybook Weaver*, an integrated graphics and word processing program for children, was on display. To make a picture you choose from a variety of landscapes—skies, mountains, rivers, yards— and then you choose people, animals, buildings and the like to fill out the image. It is all clip art. Then you can add text to the pictures and with a bunch of these you create a story. Unfamiliar with this kind of software, Joe Pearce was taken aback. As he watched the presenter flip through a variety of prefab landscapes, his eyes filled with tears. "This isn't imagination or creativity, it's just . . ." and he was overcome with sadness. Drawing pictures and making up stories is something that most children take to with little prompting. If the software does it for them, are we stealing away the image-making capacity from children? Does *Storybook Weaver* just encourage children to become consumers of externally produced images?

Let us make it acceptable for parents and teachers to just say no to significant amounts of television and computers until children enter adolescence. Childhood is short enough; there is no need to hasten its demise with exposure to soul-depleting electronic media. In my household, we figure it is a good idea to immunize our children against the onslaught of mass culture by allowing our children three or four hours of combined television or computer use per week. This avoids the forbidden fruit effect and gives us good material for dinnertime conversations. And in place of electronic media, let us work for dynamic classrooms and safe neighborhoods. I say we start a new movement called *Take Back the Afternoon* that advocates for real, old-fashioned play, at least a couple of days a week. Perhaps we can create our own bandwagon.

Periodical Bibliography

The following articles have been selected to supplement the diverse views presented in this chapter.

Chronicle of Higher Education	"Freshmen Arrive Bearing Gadgets and Great Expectations," September 22, 2006.
Shelia R. Cotton and Shameeka M. Jelenewicz	"A Disappearing Digital Divide Among College Students? Peeling Away the Layers of the Digital Divide," *Social Science Computer Review*, Winter 2006.
Bob Doyle	"Crossing the Digital Divide," *EContent*, September 2006.
Sue Ferguson	"How Computers Make Our Kids Stupid," *Maclean's*, June 6, 2005.
Lisa Guernsey	"When Gadgets Get in the Way," *New York Times*, August 19, 2004.
Wendy Haig	"Bring the World Together, Online," *Business Week Online*, November 8, 2006. www.businessweek.com.
Vicky Hallett	"Teaching with Tech," *U.S. News & World Report*, October 17, 2005.
Edward Miller	"Fighting Technology for Toddlers," *Education Digest*, November 2005.
Peter D. Stephenson and Joan Peckham	"Seeing Is Believing: Using Computer Graphics to Enthuse Students," *IEEE Computer Graphics & Applications*, November/December 2006.
Mark Toner	"Back to the Future," *Teacher Magazine*, May/June 2006.
Patrick Tucker	"Digitally Enhanced Teaching," *Futurist*, July/August 2005.
Jessica E. Vascellaro	"Saying No to School Laptops," *Wall Street Journal*, August 31, 2006.

Should the Government Regulate Technology?

Chapter Preface

On July 19, 2006, President George W. Bush vetoed the Stem Cell Research Enhancement Act of 2005, a piece of legislation that would have amended the Public Health Service Act to permit federal funding of stem cell research on human embryos discarded by fertility clinics. The president, in applying his veto, affirmed his view that tampering with human embryos was morally unconscionable and would bring science and ethics into a conflict that would have serious consequences for the nation. His decision was not unexpected. During a televised address in 2001 Bush had made clear how he would react to proposed stem cell legislation, when he stated:

> I ... believe human life is a sacred gift from our Creator. I worry about a culture that devalues life, and believe as your President I have an important obligation to foster and encourage respect for life in America and throughout the world. And while we're all hopeful about the potential of this research, no one can be certain that the science will live up to the hope it has generated.

The president maintained this view throughout his administration, promising to veto any legislation that upset the delicate balance his policy struck between science and conscience.

Supporters of Bush's policy believe—as the president does—that the government's chief executive has a duty to provide ethical as well as political leadership for America. Passing judgment on a subject as contentious as embryonic stem cell research, which involves the destruction of human embryos, the president had to weigh not only the implications of such annihilation, but he also had to gauge how divided the public was on the issue. In the case of the Stem Cell Research Enhancement Act, President Bush had to stand against a Congress that favored the legislation. Family Research Council president Tony Perkins, who attended the veto signing, championed the president's decision, stating, "Rather than defend human dignity, for the first time in U.S. history a majority of senators approved legislation to use taxpayers' money for research requiring the destruction of human life. The President is absolutely right to veto this legislation."

The government restriction on funding embryonic stem cell research will have repercussions in the scientific community and the country at large. Whatever promise embryonic stem cell therapies might have for curing debilitating illnesses and otherwise improving human health will either have to be revealed in foreign nations with no set proscriptions against this research, or it will have to be developed in American institutions that do not rely on government money. According to some critics, this fact has prompted many top-notch American scientists to immigrate to countries where embryo research is encouraged and well funded. Senator Dianne Feinstein of California told Congress, "Because of President Bush's restrictions, some of our best and brightest scientists are leaving the United States. . . . Researchers are attracted by the federal funding provided in at least ten other nations—Germany, Finland, France, Sweden, United Kingdom, South Korea, Singapore, Israel, China, and Australia. These investments total hundreds of millions of dollars that are already producing tangible progress." Feinstein and her supporters argue that this "brain drain" will prove detrimental as America loses its scientific edge in this burgeoning field of research.

As the battle over embryonic stem cell experimentation illustrates, the government's regulation of science is a hotly debated issue in the United States. In the following chapter, experts dispute the pros and cons of government oversight of other up-and-coming technologies.

> *"Allowing [telecommunications] companies to levy a toll on information providers is not just a blow to consumer choice—it's a blow to democracy."*

The Government Should Support Internet Neutrality

The New Republic

Telecommunications companies should not be allowed to give preferential treatment to Internet businesses or content providers, argues the New Republic *in the following viewpoint. According to the weekly political opinion magazine, by allowing telecom giants to charge providers a fee to have their Web sites broadcast—and perhaps even broadcast faster than other sites—these industries can upset fair competition among Internet businesses or perhaps tamper with free speech by downgrading the broadcast speed of less-than-compliant Web sites. The* New Republic *concludes that the telecom industry should maintain Internet neutrality to keep the marketplace of goods and ideas fair to all.*

As you read, consider the following questions:

1. As the *New Republic* states, what government body exempted Internet telecommunications providers from the 1934 regulations concerning "preferential treatment" practices?

2. What businesses and organizations does the author say are supportive of "net neutrality?"

3. For what reason is the *New Republic* skeptical of the Washington Post's argument that telecom providers would lose customers if they gave preferential treatment to specific Web sites?

I magine you were choosing whether to buy a book from Amazon.com or Barnes and Noble's website, and you knew that Amazon's site would load much faster, allowing you to scan books and sample their content much more easily. Or imagine that Fox.com's streaming video came up instantly and CNN.com's balked. Or that whitehouse.gov loaded quickly while the site of a contentious political magazine was plagued by delays. That is what your Internet experience could be like if Congress doesn't require the big cable and telephone companies that control access to the Web to observe what is called "net neutrality."

Under the original rules put in place in 1934, telecommunications companies can't give preferential treatment to one set of outgoing calls over another by, say, offering static-free calling to one company's telemarketers but not another's. The same rules initially applied to the Internet. Telecom companies couldn't charge website proprietors to have their content sent to consumers more expeditiously. But, [in] August [2005], George W. Bush's Federal Communications Commission (FCC) exempted telecoms that provide Internet connections from these restrictions, dealing a blow to both entrepreneurship and political discourse.

A Surcharge for Speed

Content providers from Google and Amazon to Daily Kos [political analysis blog] and TNR [The*New Republic*] Online currently pay Web-hosting companies to put their content on the Internet. Consumers then access that content via Internet

Moving Away from a Competitive Marketplace

[This is] what would happen if discrimination reigned on the Internet: a transformation from a market where innovation rules to one where deal-making rules. Or, a market where firms rush to make exclusive agreements with AT&T and Verizon instead of trying to improve their products. There's a deeper point here: When who you know matters more than anything, the market is no longer meritocratic [ruled by competition and talent] and consequently becomes less efficient. At the extreme, a market where centralized actors pick favorites isn't a market at all, but a planned economy.

Tim Wu, Slate, May 1, 2006. www.slate.com.

service providers, such as Comcast and Verizon. Under the new FCC guidelines, those companies will be able to charge content providers a fee to deliver their content to consumers and, in particular, an additional surcharge to deliver their content to consumers more quickly—that is, they will be able to create a faster toll lane on the information superhighway. If they want, the telecoms can favor their own services and penalize competitors—for instance, voice over Internet protocol companies like Vonage—by denying them faster service. They can even charge lucrative fees to companies for exclusive access to the fast lane at the expense of their competitors, giving, for example, L.L. Bean an advantage over Lands' End. And, by making the fast lane prohibitively expensive, they can force start-up ventures and noncommercial providers (like blogs) onto the bumpy dirt roads of the Internet.

Net neutrality would prohibit all of this. Telecoms could make money the way they always have—by charging homes and businesses for an Internet connection—but they couldn't make money from the content providers themselves. That is a perfectly reasonable proposition, and it has won support from Amazon and eBay, as well as the Christian Coalition and MoveOn.org. But the big cable and phone companies, backed by the Competitive Enterprise Institute, Grover Norquist's Americans for Tax Reform, and a host of well-heeled lobbyists—including former Clinton Press Secretary Mike McCurry—have adamantly resisted net neutrality. [In June 2006] they defeated a House measure, sponsored by Representative Ed Markey, to bar discrimination on the Internet. The battle now moves to the Senate, where Olympia Snowe [of Maine] and Byron Dorgan [of North Dakota] are putting forward a similar proposal.

Filtering Ideas

Opponents of net neutrality claim that telecoms need the extra money from surcharges and exclusive deals to fund new investments in cable and DSL. But the companies can still make money by charging homes and businesses higher fees for faster or more dependable services. Opponents also claim that, if consumers don't like what they are getting from one Internet service provider, they can simply switch. "If one broadband provider slowed access to fringe bloggers," *The Washington Post* opined, "the provider would lose customers." But, with the industry dominated by a handful of companies, the typical American has a choice of only two providers. And changing services often means losing an e-mail address and facing new connection charges.

Most important, as Stanford Law Professor Lawrence Lessig has argued, the Internet is not only a tool for economic growth, it is also a public commons for the exchange of ideas. It is where Americans can not only search for the best deal on a new digital camera, but also debate the country's future. Unlike the telephone, it is a medium in which thousands, even millions, of people can participate in the same discussion at the same time. Unlike television, it is interactive. But it can't function optimally if content is prioritized or filtered by telecom companies. Allowing companies to levy a toll on information providers is not just a blow to consumer choice—it's a blow to democracy.

▌ *"Don't regulate what isn't broken."*

The Government Should Oppose Internet Neutrality

The Wall Street Journal

The Wall Street Journal *is an international newspaper with the second-largest circulation of all newspapers in the United States. In the following viewpoint the newspaper contends that Internet neutrality is a "solution in search of a problem." The* Journal *contends that the Internet has blossomed without government regulation and that imposing laws on telecommunications providers to ensure that no impartial treatment is given to Web sites is wrongheaded. Enacting laws will only tie up the courts with litigation and stifle innovation on the part of telecommunications companies that will no longer take risks for fear of lawsuits, the newspaper claims.*

As you read, consider the following questions:

1. In the *Wall Street Journal*'s view, how does the FCC's list of "Net neutrality" entitlements conflict with its concern over consumer welfare?

2. Why does the author find it odd that Web operators such as Google and Microsoft support Internet neutrality?

3. Why have service providers such as AOL adopted a more "Internet-centric" method of doing business, in the *Wall Street Journal's* opinion?

If ever there was a solution in search of a problem, "Net neutrality" is it. Sometime recently, someone got up on the wrong side of bed and decided that the freedom that has been the hallmark of the Internet now threatens to destroy it.

Suddenly the Internet service providers, which you always thought were there to let you get onto the Net, are going to keep you off it unless the government imposes new laws and regulations. Congressional hearings have been held. Vint Cerf, Internet progenitor and now Google evangelist, evangelizes. Thus has the cause of Net neutrality in its current incarnation become a new and ardent crusade of the political left.

Net neutrality is generally billed as a way of reining in Internet service providers (typically phone and cable companies), some of whom have made noises about charging content companies extra fees for guaranteeing priority to certain kinds of services. Net neutrality is supposed to save us—and Google and Yahoo—from this supposedly unconscionable behavior. Its effect would be more damaging.

No Regulation Means More Innovation

It's worth putting this zealotry in a broader historical context. In the decade or so since the commercialization of the Internet began in earnest, the number of users, the speed of their connections and the variety of things they can do on the Net have all rushed forward. Blissfully, but not coincidentally, all this has been accomplished with a light regulatory touch. Excepting pornography and gambling, no bureaucrats have decided what services could be provided over the Internet, or who could offer them or how they could charge for them.

"A Plane with Empty Seats"

Proponents of Net neutrality . . . tend to ignore the fact that network capacity use and the profit motive will provide very powerful checks on overly restrictive carrier activities. Carriers make money only by carrying more traffic. "Capacity utilization" is one of the most important concepts in the networking business. A broadband network without subscribers is like a plane with empty seats: a recipe for financial disaster. BSPs [broadband service providers] will *not* want to restrict traffic flows or encumber Net-surfing activities for fear of diminished capacity use as frustrated consumers "consume" less of those networks, or leave the network altogether. That is why cable operators do not configure their set-top boxes to meddle with consumer access to traditional television stations. Even though they might have the technical capability to restrict the stations consumers watch or even when they watch them, cable operators understand that their video customer base will grow only if they expand the range of viewing options, not curtail or artificially limit them.

Adam D. Thierer, Cato Institute, Policy Analysis, *January 12, 2004.*

The result has been rich and diverse. Web surfers can make phone calls—sometimes free, sometimes for a fee. They can legally listen to music, either free, by subscription or by paying per song. They can watch some network television shows online—again, some are free and supported by ads; others charge per program.

Some of the service ideas have been bad, and failed. Some are wonderful. But many would never have been tried if the Federal Communications Commission [FCC] had been able to tell businesses whom they could charge, how much or how little, or what they could or couldn't sell on the Net. Freedom, in other words, has been the Web surfer's friend.

Enter Net neutrality, which has so far found its only official expression in a nonbinding policy statement issued by the FCC [in 2005]. The FCC statement says, "consumers are *entitled*" (our emphasis) to the "content," "applications" and "devices" of their choice on the Internet. They are also "entitled to competition among network providers, application and service providers, and content providers."

Endless Haggling over Rules

Take a moment to pause over this expansive list of "entitlements." If we take the FCC at its word, access to online pornography is now a right, even though in a different context the FCC is increasingly preoccupied with policing "decency" standards on television. We'd have thought FCC Chairman Kevin Martin would find all that entitlement talk a little embarrassing, given his campaign for decency standards.

But at least the FCC's guidelines were just that—guidelines. Increasingly, and with the backing both of the Moveon .org crowd and "Don't Be Evil" Google, a movement is afoot to give these entitlements the force of law. Congressman Ed Markey [of Massachusetts] has introduced a bill to "save the Internet" by codifying Net neutrality principles in law. The FCC would be charged with enforcing "non-discrimination" and "openness" rules.

Under a law like this—variations are floating around both houses of Congress—the country could look forward to years of litigation about the extent and nature of the rules. When the dust settled we'd have a new set of regulations that could span the range of possible activities on the Net. What's more, the rules aren't likely to stop with the phone and cable companies that have Mr. Markey and his friends at Moveon.org so exercised.

Non-discrimination cases could well be brought against Net neutrality backers like Google—say, for placing a competitor too low in their search results. Google's recent complaint that Microsoft's new operating system was anti-competitive is a foretaste of what the battles over a "neutral" Net would look like. Yet Google and other Web site operators have jumped on the Net neutrality bandwagon lest they have to pay a fee to get a guaranteed level of service from a Verizon or other Internet service provider. They don't seem to comprehend the legal and political danger they'll face once they open the neutrality floodgates. We'd have thought Microsoft of all companies would have learned this lesson from its anti-trust travails, but it too has now hired lawyers to join the Net neutrality lobby.

A Fix Without a Problem

All the recent scare-mongering about the coming ruination of the Internet is cloaked in rhetoric about how recent court rulings and regulatory actions by the FCC have undermined certain "protections." This is mostly bluster. Companies like AOL did not migrate from a "walled garden" to a more-open, Internet-centric model because of mandates from Washington but because the alternative was extinction.

Given the impulse on the left to regulate anything that moves, perhaps the real surprise here is that it's taken this long for someone to seriously suggest the Net will wither in the absence of a federal regulatory apparatus. "Don't ruin the Internet" is a slogan with a lot of merit. But it comes with a modern corollary, which is "Don't regulate what isn't broken."

"Adequate government oversight of nanotechnology is an essential part of 'getting it right.'"

The Government Should Regulate Nanotechnology More Strictly

J. Clarence Davies

J. Clarence Davies is the senior advisor to the Project on Emerging Technologies at the Woodrow Wilson International Center for Scholars. In the following viewpoint, Davies argues that nanotechnology—the production and use of materials at a molecular level—is a field of enormous promise and potential dangers. Because of the unknown risks of putting this technology to use in manufacturing consumer items, Davies believes nanotechnology should be more strictly regulated by the government. According to Davies, existing laws are not enough to protect the public from this emerging technology, and therefore the federal government will have to enact new statutes tailored to the possible hazards.

J. Clarence Davies, testimony: "Developments in Nanotechnology," U.S. Senate Committee on Commerce, Science and Transportation hearing February 15, 2006. Reproduced by permission of the author.

As you read, consider the following questions:

1. Based on past experience and focus group surveys, what does Davies fear the public will do if nanotechnology is not regulated by the government?

2. What does the author believe are the three faults of using existing laws to govern nanotechnology?

3. According to Davies, what problem exists in trusting companies to perform voluntary testing on their nano-tech products?

Nanotechnology is still very new and it is full of promise. It may offer solutions to many of the most serious problems our society faces. It offers the hope of significant breakthroughs in areas such as medicine, clean energy and water, environmental remediation, and green manufacturing. However, we currently know little about the short- and long-term effects of nanotechnology on human health or the environment.

Additionally, the public's views of nanotechnology remain largely unformed. The vast majority of people have never heard of nanotechnology, though it is anticipated that they will learn about the technology as applications emerge and as products enter the market. For this reason, we now have a unique opportunity "to get it right"—to introduce a major new technology without incurring significant public opposition and without gambling with the health of citizens, workers, consumers, or the environment.

A lot depends on our ability to "get it right." If we fail, we run a double risk. First, we run the risk of unanticipated harm to health and the environment. Second, we run the risk of public rejection of the technology. Our past experiences—with agricultural biotechnology, nuclear power, and asbestos, just to name a few—illustrate how tragic either of these scenarios could be. Industry, as well as the general public, has a big stake in ensuring that nanotechnology is developed responsibly from the start.

Adequate government oversight of nanotechnology is an essential part of "getting it right." The public does not trust industry to regulate itself. Past experience, as well as surveys and focus groups, show that if the public does not think that the government is exercising adequate regulatory oversight of a potentially hazardous new technology then it will mistrust and likely reject that technology. If this happens, literally billions of dollars of investment by government and industry in nanotechnology research and development may be jeopardized.

To date, the National Nanotechnology Coordinating Office (NNCO) has maintained that the federal agencies have adequate statutory authority to deal with nanotechnology. E. Clayton Teague, director of the NNCO, has said that: "Until we have good, solid, scientifically validated information that would indicate significant inadequacies in existing regulatory authorities, additional regulations would just be unnecessarily burdensome." This is an insufficient response to the challenge, and, I believe, misleading to both the public and industry. By overstating the case for regulatory adequacy, one shifts risks onto corporate investors, shareholders, and the exposed public.

Possible Health Threats

The analysis in my report [*Managing the Effects of Nanotechnology*, 2006] clearly shows that the existing regulatory structure for nanotechnology is not adequate. It suffers from three types of problems: (1) gaps in statutory authority, (2) inadequate resources, and (3) a poor fit between some of the regulatory programs and the characteristics of nanotechnology.

(1) The gaps in statutory authority are most obvious with respect to two of the most common uses of nanomaterials—

Toxicity Concerns About Nanotechnology

One of the reasons for concern about nanoparticles' toxicity has to do with simple physics. For instance, as a particle shrinks, the ratio of its surface area to its mass rises. A material that's seemingly inert in bulk thus has a larger surface area as a collection of nanoparticles, which can lead to greater reactivity. For certain applications, this is an advantage; but it can also mean greater toxicity. "The normal measure of toxicity is the mass of the toxin, but with nanomaterials, you need a whole different set of metrics," says Vicki Colvin, a professor of chemistry at Rice University in Houston and a leading expert on nanomaterials.

Beyond the question of increased reactivity, the sheer tininess of nanoparticles is itself a cause for concern. Toxicologists have known for years that relatively small particles could create health problems when inhaled.

Philip E. Ross, Technology Review,
May/June 2006.

cosmetics and consumer products. In both cases, there is essentially no statutory authority to review the health and safety of these products. In both cases, the principle is caveat emptor—let the buyer beware. In both areas, there is large potential for human exposure to nanomaterials. A wide variety of nano-based consumer products have already begun to enter the market as sporting goods, clothing, cleaning materials, and kitchen appliances. Similarly, nano-based cosmetic products already range from skin creams to spray-on foot deodorizers, all with significant exposure potential (dermal, inhalation, and ingestion) and little publicly available risk data.

A more subtle set of statutory problems relates to the Toxic Substances Control Act (TSCA), which many have suggested as the primary law that should be used to regulate nanotechnology. TSCA is a very weak law. . . . One weakness is particularly important in relation to nanotechnology. TSCA implicitly assumes that if there is no information on the risk of a chemical then there is no risk. In other words, the law acts as a significant disincentive to generating information on possible risks of a chemical. This is exactly the opposite of what is needed. A major reason to adequately regulate nanotechnology is to provide an incentive for generating information. There is an interaction between regulation and information. A certain amount of information is needed to make regulation work, but regulation, properly crafted, can provide an important incentive to produce health and safety information.

Lack of Experienced Overseers

(2) All of the federal regulatory programs suffer from a shortage of resources. This shortage of resources is not only related to funding levels. There is also a shortage of personnel—particularly individuals with the appropriate expertise to deal with nanotechnology. For some of the programs most relevant to nanotechnology the deficiency is so great that it raises doubts about whether the program can function at all. In 1980, The Occupational Safety and Health Administration (OSHA) had 2,950 employees, a number that was inadequate for its responsibilities then. Today, with a greatly expanded economy and workforce, OSHA has 2,208 employees, approximately 25% fewer. The Consumer Product Safety Commission (CPSC) has, since its creation, suffered from both statutory and resource problems. Today CPSC has half the staff that it had in 1980. Statutory authority without the resources for implementation will not lead to adequate oversight. . . .

No Existing Laws Are Geared to Nanotechnology

(3) None of the health and environment laws were drafted with nanotechnology in mind, and fitting nanotechnology into the existing statutory framework can be problematic. For example, many of the environmental statutes are based on an assumption that there is a direct relationship between quantity or volume on one hand and degree of risk on the other. This relationship does not hold for most nanomaterials.

In the near term, we will have to make do with current laws and programs. . . . Though voluntary programs have been put forth as an interim solution, they are not a solution over the long-term.

Voluntary programs tend to leave out the firms that most need to be regulated. Such programs also lack both transparency and accountability and thus do not contribute to public confidence in the regulatory system.

When I began working on the report, I did not believe that new legislation would be necessary. However, given all of the shortcomings of the existing system, I now believe that it is in everyone's interest to start thinking about what a new law might look like. The existing laws are not adequate. They cannot provide protection for the public, or offer a predictable marketplace for nanotechnology businesses and investors. No amount of coordination or patching is likely to fix the problem. . . .

Three Significant Questions

Since its release in January 2006, the report has attracted a good deal of attention. I have frequently been asked three questions which are worth briefly addressing here:

1. Is there any reason to believe that there are any adverse effects from nanotechnology?

2. Can't industry be trusted to test new products since it is in its best interest to do so?

3. Don't we need to wait for more information before we can regulate nanotechnology?

(1) *Adverse effects*: I am not a toxicologist, and I do not have the qualifications to address in depth the potential adverse effects of nanotechnology. However, there are three reasons to believe that such effects are likely. First, every technology of the scope of nanotechnology has had adverse effects. The idea that nanotechnology could be completely innocuous flies in the face of what we have learned over many years of dealing with technological innovation.

Second, many decades of studying exposure to fine particles—in the workplace and the environment in general—have shown that inhaling fine (and possibly nanometer-sized) particles can be harmful. Third, on-going research into the health implications of engineered nanomaterials raises many questions and concerns. For instance, we know that:

- Nanometer-scale particles behave differently from larger-sized particles in the lungs—possibly moving to other organs in the body;

- The surface of some nano-structured particles is associated with toxicity—rather than the more usually measured mass concentration; and

- Conventional toxicity tests do not seem to work well with nanomaterials such as carbon nanotubes. . . .

The debate over how safe nanotechnology is, and how risk should be governed, must be conducted in the knowledge that nanotechnologies—or the specific applications of nanotechnology—are diverse. Some will present a far greater risk to health and the environment than others. . . .

(2) *Voluntary testing*: It is in the interest of most manufacturers to do some tests of their products. A number of companies have a reputation of exceeding current regulatory re-

quirements in regards to product testing, and no manufacturer wants its customers or workers to be adversely affected by its products. However, testing, when done, is largely for short-term acute effects and not for long-term effects, such as cancer, mutagenesis, and environmental effects. Testing for long-term health and environmental effects can be expensive and, if there is some adverse effect, it is unlikely that the effect will ever be associated with the particular product. Thus it can be tempting not to do such testing, if not required.

(3) *Information and regulation*: We do need more information before an adequate oversight system can succeed. But it is not too early to start thinking and talking about the outlines of such a system. It is not too early because nanotechnology products are being commercialized now, and the regulatory system must deal with them. A survey by EmTech Research of companies working in the field of nanotechnology has identified approximately 80 nanotechnology consumer products, and over 600 nanotechnology-based raw materials, intermediate components and industrial equipment items that are used by manufacturers. Experts at the Project on Emerging Nanotechnologies believe that the number of nanotechnology consumer products on the market worldwide is actually larger than the EmTech data suggest.

Furthermore, it also is not too early to start thinking and talking about an oversight system because knowing what a regulatory structure will look like can provide important guidance about what information is needed. Given the realities of the legislative process, it could be years before new legislation is enacted.

> "The nascent [nanotech] industry faces threats from those who believe government should solve problems before they occur."

The Government Should Not Regulate Nanotechnology More Strictly

Sonia Arrison

In the following viewpoint, Sonia Arrison claims that nanotechnology is a growing field with a variety of applications. Although the new field may have risks, Arrison warns that focusing on unknown consequences can stifle innovation. Therefore, she states that the government should refrain from enacting regulation and let the scientific and production communities determine how nanotechnology should progress. Sonia Arrison is the director of Technology Studies at the Pacific Research Institute in California.

As you read, consider the following questions:

1. How can nanotechnology be used to cure disease, according to Arrison?

2. What prediction does the author cite in reference to the global marketplace potential of nanotechnology in 2015?

3. As Arrison reports, how can overregulation of nanotechnology possibly lead to underregulation?

Anyone who purchased clear sunscreen or wore stain-resistant pants during the holidays was probably enjoying the benefits of commercialized nanotechnology. While nanotech advances are exciting, some observers dangerously press for greater government oversight in the sector.

Nanotechnology, the manipulation of matter at the molecular level, can create better materials, such as stronger metals and better paints. It also opens the door for self-replicating devices and particles so small that they may enter the bloodstream to help cure disease. This revolution, like any new technology, can be deployed for beneficial or nefarious purposes.

Overestimating the Risks

In a report released [in January 2006], environmental policy analyst J. Clarence Davies argued for greater regulation of nanotechnology. America's current laws, he says, "either suffer from major shortcomings of legal authority, or from a gross lack of resources, or both." The problem, according to Davies, is that current laws "provide a very weak basis for identifying and protecting the public from potential risk, especially as nanotechnologies become more complex in structure and function and the applications become more diverse."

Of course, Davies also admits that "we know little about possible adverse effects of nanotechnology." That's partly because of the nascent status of the technology and perhaps also because the risks aren't that high. Even government officials seemed surprised at the suggestion of new regulations.

Clayton Teague, director of the National Nanotechnology Coordination Office, told the Associated Press that "until we have information that there are truly inadequacies in existing regulations, any additional regulations beyond what we already would have would be burdensome to industry and the advancement of the field."

It's encouraging to see national policy makers taking such a reasonable stand. Perhaps that's because they know that advances in nanotechnology will bring greater economic opportunities and tax dollars.

Indeed, it has been estimated that by 2015, the global marketplace for products that use the technology will reach US$1 trillion and employ two million workers. The technology is so promising that the state of California recently released a report brainstorming on how to create a successful Nano-Valley, similar to Silicon Valley, which didn't face regulatory threats in its infancy.

Regulation Paradox

For his part, Davies argues that current levels of government oversight could create distrust and lead to a "public rejection of the technology." While government rules sometimes have a legitimizing effect, that's a poor reason to support them. Over-regulation comes with serious dangers too.

Not only can too many regulations strangle innovation in the cradle, but over-regulation can ironically cause under-regulation, leading to safety hazards. In *Forward to the Future*, a Pacific Research Institute report, law professor and celebrity blogger Glenn Reynolds discusses this problem.

"When statutes require especially stringent regulations, administrators will tend not to issue regulations at all. Extraordinarily strict rules on workplace toxins, for example, have led to a failure by the Occupational Safety and Health Administration (OSHA) to address all but a tiny minority of chemicals believed to be toxic." And of course, government rules tend to discourage the creation of private-sector solutions.

A Responsible and Protective Field of Study

Nanotech companies are led by socially conscious scientists, managers and investors. Nanotechnology employs many of the most environmentally and safety oriented professionals in the business and scientific world. They all have wives, children and grandchildren. That alone makes them fundamentally committed, almost to a fault, to creating and manufacturing safe and environmentally sound nanoproducts.

Industry scientists jump on and solve any issue relating to any possible safety risks in weeks. . . . In addition, nanotechnology supports an industry association, the Nanobusiness Alliance, . . . with a platform of responsible safety and efficacy promotion that has testified before Congress on safety and environmental issues. In sum, nanotechnology worldwide involves many of the most concerned citizens on this planet.

Alan B. Shalleck, PRWeb, October 16, 2006. www.prweb.com.

The Freedom to Be Innovative

The scientific community is well aware of the potential dangers with nano-scale particles. The public will be glad to know that the discussion over proper methods is thriving and developing in tandem with the technology. In addition, concerned groups such as the Foresight Institute in California have released guidelines for self-regulation modeled on the extensive experience in biotechnology where there has been great technical progress and little danger to public safety.

Nanotechnology holds much promise for advances in a number of areas such as material science and medicine, but the nascent industry faces threats from those who believe government should solve problems before they occur. Nanotech scientists must be free to develop their products, as well as the rules that govern their development, in order to reap the rewards and protect society from potential pitfalls. The best approach is the light regulation that already exists, combined with a strong scientific culture of self-regulation.

"The United States should prohibit all human cloning, regardless of its aim."

The Government Should Ban Therapeutic Cloning

Leon R. Kass

Leon R. Kass is a professor in the Committee on Social Thought and the College at the University of Chicago and chairman of the President's Council on Bioethics. In the following viewpoint, Kass argues that all cloning threatens the dignity of human procreation. Human cloning is, to him, an abomination, and therapeutic cloning—the use of human embryo stem cells to treat diseases—is an unproven and possibly unnecessary field of research. Even worse, contends Kass, while therapeutic cloning seems to hold out hope to millions of people suffering from debilitating illnesses, such manipulation of genetic coding will not stop at the treatment of disease and will inevitably lead to predesigned children.

As you read, consider the following questions:

1. As Kass states, what "act" makes cloning to produce children and cloning for therapeutic reasons similar?

2. What three reasons does the author give to distrust the promise and necessity of therapeutic cloning?

3. Which foreign bodies and governments does Kass say have banned human cloning in all its forms?

Opposition to cloning to produce children is practically unanimous in America: The vast majority of Americans oppose it. Most research scientists agree that it should be banned. Nearly every member of Congress has condemned it. Cloning not only carries high risks of bodily harm to the cloned child, but it also threatens the dignity of human procreation, giving one generation unprecedented genetic control over the next. It is the first step toward a eugenic world in which children become objects of manipulation and products of will.

Yet legislation that would have banned cloning failed to pass the Senate [in 2002]. Partisans on both sides of the cloning debate sought to entangle it with the larger debate about stem cell and embryo research. Disentangling the two debates is the key to passing responsible legislation that would prohibit this practice in the United States.

All Cloning Involves Human Embryos

We first need to be clear about the facts. All human cloning begins with the same act: the production of a cloned human embryo. Cloning to produce children would involve the implantation of such embryos in a woman's body and their development to birth; cloning for biomedical research, in contrast, involves the dissection of these embryos to obtain stem cells (and, someday perhaps, the harvesting of fetal tissues and organs).

The political controversy is whether both or only the first of these uses of cloning should be prohibited—and whether, as a practical and moral matter, it is possible to stop cloning to produce children while allowing cloning for research.

The debate so far has been inadequate and wrongly focused. Supporters of cloning for research have often tried to confuse the issue by euphemistic distortion—claiming that the production of cloned embryos is not really cloning, that the embryos produced are not really embryos at all. At the same time, they have falsely characterized a ban on cloning for research as a ban on all embryo and stem cell research.

Opponents of cloning research, meanwhile, have been preoccupied with putting a stop to the destruction of embryos and so have failed to focus on what is unique about all human cloning: the expanded power to manipulate nascent human life and thus to master the very technique that will make cloning to produce children possible. Were this danger better understood, opposition to the practice would mount.

No Reason to Suspect Benefits of Therapeutic Cloning

It is true that cloning research offers hope, however speculative, for understanding and treating disease. Yet we should not deceive ourselves about the value and necessity of such research: there is virtually no precedent in animal work that demonstrates the unique benefits of creating and exploiting cloned embryos; we have only just begun to understand existing embryonic stem cells; and promising results with adult stem cells, if confirmed, may obviate altogether the putative need for cloned stem cells.

It is also true that the ethics of embryo research is relevant to the cloning debate. Cloning research would require the routine production of embryos solely as a source for experimentation. It would require large numbers of human eggs and invite the exploitation of egg donors. And legislation that allowed creating cloned embryos for research while criminalizing their implantation to create cloned children would mandate, by law, the destruction of nascent human life.

A Staggering Number of Human Embryos

There are more than 100 million Americans, according to the National Academy of Sciences [NAS], who might one day benefit from therapeutic cloning if all the high hopes for it panned out. Each therapeutic cloning attempt would require one human egg. If it takes 100 tries per patient for a cloned embryonic stem cell line to be successfully created, therapeutic cloning will never become a widely available therapy in medicine's armamentarium because there will never be enough eggs.

Do the math: 100 million patients at 100 eggs each would mean that biotechnologists would need access to at least 10 billion eggs just to treat the Americans the NAS has identified as having degenerative conditions that might respond positively to stem cell therapy.

Wesley J. Smith, National Right to Life News, *October 2003.*

One Clone Leads to Another

The central issue in the cloning debate, however, and the primary reason to support a ban or moratorium on all human cloning, is this: it threatens the dignity of human procreation. Concern about this threat should lead us to oppose all cloning, including cloning for research.

Human cloning must be seen in the context of our growing powers over human reproduction augmented by new knowledge of the human genome. Science already permits us to screen human embryos in vitro for thousands of human genes. These include not only those that have markers for dread diseases, but also soon genes responsible for other human traits: not just sex, height or skin color but even intelligence, temperament or sexual orientation.

Genetic selection of embryos is today a growing industry. Some experts hail assisted reproduction as the route to genetically sound babies. While directed genetic change of human embryos (even for therapeutic purposes) may be a long way off, it has been accomplished in primates in the laboratory. It would be naive to believe that cloning children will be confined to infertile couples and that cloning research will be confined to studies of disease.

Viewed in this larger context, the production of cloned embryos for any purpose is a significant leap in transforming procreation into a form of manufacture. The embryo created by cloning would be the first human embryo to have its genetic identity selected in advance, the first embryo whose makeup is not the unpredictable result of uniting sperm and egg. It is precisely this genetic control that makes cloned embryos appealing and useful.

It Is Time to Enact a Ban

But we should not be deceived: saying yes to cloned embryos, even for research, means saying yes, at least in principle, to an ever-expanding genetic mastery of one generation over the next. Once cloned human embryos exist in laboratories, the eugenic revolution will have begun.

It is these concerns that have caused many countries to prohibit all human cloning, both for reproduction and research. Germany, Italy, France, Norway, Australia and other democracies, many of which support embryo research, have said no to this practice. The European Parliament, hardly an arm of the religious right, has also called for the prohibition of all human cloning.

Our country should do the same. The United States should prohibit all human cloning, regardless of its aim—or, at the very least, ban it for several years.

Such a policy would allow time to consider the real significance of crossing this crucial moral boundary. It would allow time for other areas of stem cell research, both adult and embryonic, to proceed. It would provide the most effective safeguard against the production of cloned children by stopping cloning before it starts. And it would allow the national debate to continue.

If we do nothing now, human cloning will happen here, and we will have acquiesced in its arrival. It is time for Congress to act.

> "Not only will the present generation not get medical relief from stem cell research, it is beginning to look as if our children's generation will not either."

The Government Should Not Ban Therapeutic Cloning

Michael Gazzaniga

In the following viewpoint, Michael Gazzaniga argues that therapeutic cloning (or biomedical cloning) should not be restricted by a government ban. Gazzaniga rejects notions that the human embryo cells used in therapeutic experiments are nascent life. In his view, these cells cannot grow into humans without complex biological interactions and environmental influences. To deny their use in medical treatments, he argues, is to deny living humans the possibility of overcoming disabling illnesses and genetic diseases through stem cell manipulation. Michael Gazzaniga is the director of the Center for Cognitive Neuroscience at Dartmouth College in New Hampshire. He has served on the President's Council on Bioethics since 2002.

Michael Gazzaniga, "All Clones Are Not the Same," *New York Times*, February 16, 2006, p. A33. Copyright © 2006 by The New York Times Company. Reprinted with permission.

As you read, consider the following questions:

1. According to Gazzaniga, what was the result of the President's Council on Bioethics vote regarding cloning?

2. For scientists, what have been the repercussions of President Bush's call for a ban on all forms of cloning, in the author's view?

3. As Gazzaniga reports, what did the late Ira Black do in New Jersey to push stem cell research forward despite the government"s indecision on the issue?

It has been weeks since President [George W.] Bush's [2006] State of the Union speech, and I have not heard any outcry over his policy statement on cloning: "Tonight I ask you to pass legislation to prohibit the most egregious abuses of medical research: human cloning in all its forms." I can only guess that this means the public doesn't care, or doesn't understand what Mr. Bush means by this, or agrees with his nonsensical concept of what "human" means, or that somehow the [2005] stem cell scandal in South Korea [in which results of a doctor's stem cell research and cloning experiments were found to be faked] has led to widespread agreement that we should just give up on such research. Any of these possibilities would be a mistake, not just for American science, but for the very human life the president seeks to protect.

Calling human cloning in all its forms an "egregious abuse" is a serious mischaracterization. This makes it sound as if the medical community is out there cloning people, which is simply not true. The phrase "in all of its forms" is code, a way of conflating very different things: reproductive cloning and biomedical cloning.

The volatile issue has been debated again and again, and the president's own largely conservative Bioethics Council (of which I am a member) in 2002 made a big distinction between the two forms of cloning. We voted unanimously to ban reproductive cloning—the kind of cloning that seeks to replicate a human being. We cited many reasons, from biomedical risk to religious concerns to the flat-out weirdness of the idea. But in fact human cloning has not been attempted, nor is it in the works; so it's a theoretical ban in the first place, like banning marriage between robots.

At the same time, the council had differing views on biomedical cloning, including stem cell research. Seven of the 17 voting members voted to allow scientists to proceed with the practice, pending regulations, while three more voted for a moratorium until such regulations were written. Thus, the majority, 10 of the 17, did not call for a ban on biomedical cloning—and this was our advice to the president. Obviously, he ignored it.

Cells Are Not People

Why is there a persistent difference of views on the morality of biomedical cloning? The president's view is consistent with the reductive idea that there is an equivalence between a bunch of molecules in a lab and a beautifully nurtured and loved human who has been shaped by a lifetime of experiences and discovery. His view is a form of the "DNA is destiny" story.

Yet all modern research reveals that DNA must undergo thousands if not millions of interactions at both the molecular and experiential level to grow and develop a brain and become a person. It is the journey that makes a human, not the car. Unfortunately, the president rejected the advice of his own counselors and has kept his ban on federal financing of stem cell research for all but a handful of strains of existing lines.

The impact of his intervention with science has been severe. First, it has caused scientists at the forefront of cutting-edge research that may cure diseases and save lives to have to scramble for alternative financing. Second, the political games around stem cell research are sending scientists on wild goose chases, pursuing costly and strange alternative ideas, some of which may work in the distant future but many of which probably will not.

This search for alternatives is costly not just in dollar terms but also in time not being spent on the best research possibilities. And it represents a perversion of the scientific process: instead of science proceeding in the best way it knows, it is being used in the service of political goals. Not only will the present generation not get medical relief from stem cell research, it is beginning to look as if our children's generation will not either.

Stem Cell Research Will Proceed

In the scientific community there have obviously been strains. When the sad and pathetic story of the fraud in South Korea came to light, I couldn't help but wonder if the entire process—from the overly ambitious laboratory scientist to the overly eager editors of scientific journals—was compromised by a conscious or unconscious sense that something must keep stem cell research alive in the face of the American administration's unwavering opposition.

There have been whispered accusations in the research world that scientists and editors have become too eager to prove that stem cell research is moving ahead in other countries while America is being left behind. I think such accusations are unfounded, but I do recognize [that] the news of the scandal has probably hurt the stem cell cause.

That is the bad news. The better news is that if our government won't let biomedical science in the front door, it is going to come in through the windows. Ira Black, a leading neuroscientist who died suddenly [in January 2006], showed what medical scientists can do when they take the initiative. As the driving force behind Stem Cell Institute of New Jersey, he brought governors and state legislators to their senses by painstakingly lobbying and explaining his vision of laboratory-to-bedside stem cell research all under one roof. As a result, the State of New Jersey is moving ahead while the federal government is sitting still.

California voters, too, have anted up $3 billion for the stem cell effort, and as soon as the legal maneuvering comes to an end, that state will begin a serious program. Harvard and other institutions are also in the hunt for science and cure. At the most recent meeting of our bioethics council, Patricia Churchland, a distinguished philosopher from the University of California at San Diego, observed that throughout history, medical innovations—from vaccines to anesthesia—have been initially resisted only to later be widely accepted. It will be the same with stem cells.

The Value of Human Life

In his State of the Union speech, President Bush went on to observe that "human life is a gift from our creator—and that gift should never be discarded, devalued or put up for sale." Putting aside the belief in a "creator," the vast majority of the world's population takes a similar stance on valuing human life. What is at issue, rather, is how we are to define "human life." Look around you. Look at your loved ones. Do you see a hunk of cells or do you see something else?

Most humans practice a kind of dualism, seeing a distinction between mind and body. We all automatically confer a higher order to a developed biological entity like a human brain. We do not see cells, simple or complex—we see people, human life. That thing in a petri dish is something else. It doesn't yet have the memories and loves and hopes that accumulate over the years. Until this is understood by our politicians, the gallant efforts of so many biomedical scientists, as good as they are, will remain only stopgap measures.

Periodical Bibliography

The following articles have been selected to supplement the diverse views presented in this chapter.

Eric Bender	"Nanotech: Ultrasmall Technology, Revolutionary Impact," *PC World*, November 2006.
eWeek	"Address Nanotechnology Concerns, Experts Urge," November 15, 2006.
Global Agenda	"Cloning Embryos, Multiplying Controversies," August 13, 2004.
Thomas Haire	"We Need 'Net Neutrality' Regulation—Now!" *Response*, November 2006.
Michael Johnsen	"Nanotechnology Gets FDA Perusal," *Drug Store News*, November 6, 2006.
Johna Till Johnson	"Nuances Matter in Net Neutrality," *Network World*, November 6, 2006.
John F. Kavanaugh	"Cloning, by Whatever Name, Smells Bad: 'We Must Offer a Positive Alternative,'" *America*, June 19, 2006.
Randolph J. May	"Net Neutrality and Free Speech," *Broadcasting & Cable*, September 18, 2006.
Glen Harlan Reynolds	"The Nano Dilemma: Critics Exaggerate the Dangers. Boosters Flog the Benefits. Let's Give Nanotechnology a Chance to Develop Before We Start Taking Sides," *Popular Mechanics*, October 2006.
Space Daily	"Consumers Neutral on Risks, Benefits of Nano," December 7, 2006.
Dawn Stover	"What You're Not Being Told About Cloning," *Popular Science*, December 1, 2003.
Joni Eareckson Tada	"The Threat of Biotech: Joni Eareckson Tada Responds to Christopher Reeve and Others," *Christianity Today*, March 2003.

CHAPTER 4

Will Future Technology Improve Humanity?

Chapter Preface

Biological enhancement of human physiology is already a reality. Mood altering drugs like Prozac, for example, can make depressed individuals more optimistic and socially interactive, and anabolic steroids can help build muscle mass and increase physical performance. Such drugs are the subject of controversy, yet their use is widespread and commonplace in a society that favors serene minds and perfect bodies; however, genetically engineered bio-enhancements are another matter. The idea that nearly everything from personality traits to physical prowess may be manipulated by altering a genetic code is frightening to many people because it upsets deeply held beliefs about human nature and the proper limits of science—even if this science is not yet practicable.

Opponents of genetic enhancement condemn the possible manipulation of human characteristics for many reasons. Many criticize the science as unnatural, preferring to believe that individuals should make the most of the talents they are born with. Others fear that enhancement will be the preserve of those who can afford it, artificially adding to the class divisions already apparent in society. Still others denounce it on religious principles and contend that humans should never attempt to play God. There are even a few who argue that biotech enhancements are doomed to failure. Larry Arnhart, a political science professor and the author of *Darwinian Natural Right: The Biological Ethics of Human Nature*, states that biotechnology will always be limited in application:

> It will be limited in its technical means because complex behavioral traits are rooted in the intricate interplay of many genes, which interact with developmental contingencies and unique life histories to form brains that respond flexibly to changing circumstances. Consequently, precise technological manipulation of human nature to enhance

desirable traits while avoiding undesirable side effects will be very difficult if not impossible. Biotechnology will also be limited in its moral ends, because the motivation for biotechnological manipulations will come from the same natural desires that have always characterized human nature.

Arnhart's assertion makes all criticisms of biotechnology superfluous and deflates the claims of those who believe in the promise of enhancement.

Not everyone, however, believes that biotech research will be thwarted by the complexity of genetic interactions. Henry T. Greely, writing in the August 5, 2006, issue of the *New Scientist*, maintains that humans have constantly striven to improve themselves and that biotechnology is simply the newest phase of this ongoing project. He states, "Modern science, pushed by the drive to cure disease, is opening vast new opportunities not just to use new tools, but to change our bodies and minds. The results may include drugs that improve memory, neuro-implants that give us better or new senses, or genetic engineering for longer life." Although Greely acknowledges that biotechnology may have risks that have to be weighed against any benefits, he believes that it would be unfair to limit this science because people today cannot foresee what value may lie in the pursuit of biotech research.

Two of the authors in the following chapter take up the debate concerning genetic enhancement, revealing other facets of this controversy. The two remaining authors offer predictions about a future world in which technologies such as genetic enhancement are commonplace and humans must deal with the consequences—favorable and unfavorable—of merging humanity, science, and technology.

> *"Genetic enhancement, like other pow-*
> *erful tools we have taken from nature,*
> *should be mastered and used for the*
> *benefit of man."*

The Genetic Enhancement of Children Should Be Tolerated

David Merriman

In the following viewpoint, David Merriman, a creative writing student at Oberlin College in Ohio, argues that genetic enhancement should be mastered to benefit humankind. He believes that enhancing the traits of future generations will come with the risks that attend all great scientific endeavors, but these should not deter humans from taking advantage of the opportunities it presents. Merriman has contributed articles to Texas news periodicals.

As you read, consider the following questions:

1. What might be the medical benefits of germline therapy, according to Merriman?

2. How does Merriman refute the notion that genetic enhancement would be to blame for furthering global divisions between the haves and the have-nots?

David Merriman, "Genetic Enhancement: A 'Radical' Proposal—How Genetic Therapy Makes Less Sense Than Genetic Enhancement," Associated Content, June 14, 2006. www.associatedcontent.com. Reproduced by permission.

3. How could predetermining a child's profession be "ethically positive," in Merriman's view?

The term "genetic enhancement," perhaps stigmatized by the canonization of dystopia novels such as [Aldous Huxley's] *Brave New World* and the sensational nature of the media in reporting scientific advances, seems immediately repulsive to most Americans. Images of Alphas and Betas ruling over Epsilons and Gammas come to mind; also Nazi rule, the pseudo-science of eugenics and genetic "cleansing." With these frightening images, questions arise. What would result if such a power fell into the wrong hands? If we tamper with humanity, are we playing God? Will anything be left sacred, natural, or random? If we decide on our children's genetic makeup, will they someday regret our decision? These questions represent the firm yet arguably unfounded convictions that cloud the issue of genetic enhancement. If we, as a society, could just step back, take a few deep breaths and dissociate ourselves from our immediate emotional responses, I believe that there would appear not just a working argument for the implication of genetic enhancement, but also a strong one. It may be a surprise to some that the argument's basis is not a reframing of genetic engineering as an endeavor to increase overall quality of life within the human population, but rather, as the ethical and logical next step if we desire to progress as a human race. My proposition is that, because we exist within and find morally appropriate the exponential growth of human progress, genetic enhancement, like other powerful tools we have taken from nature, should be mastered and used for the benefit of man, to explore and conquer uncharted territory before we perish.

Types of Gene Manipulation

To begin, I will distinguish between the two different types of genetic therapy, (somatic and germline) then shift focus from genetic therapy into genetic engineering or enhancement. Somatic therapy—using somatic cells such as the liver, bone-marrow, lung, or vascular epithelium—is mostly uncontroversial. Genetically modifying somatic cells does not affect future generations. In fact, most somatic therapies will probably require repeated applications, much like ordinary pharmacological treatments. Because it is so similar to already-accepted scientific practice, current research of gene therapy is virtually exclusive to somatic gene therapy.

Germline therapy, which affects future generations, is obviously more controversial, yet in its promise holds far more enticing possibilities; also it is surprisingly easier to do. Possible therapeutic benefits from germline therapy could encompass the eradication of most genetically inheritable diseases and disorders; these include Tay-Sachs, Sickle Cell, Hemophilia, Huntington's Disease and Cystic Fibrosis, to name a few. The scale and effectiveness of germline therapy's possible benefits are almost entirely unknown, as is the approximate decade it could be administered safely throughout the public.

Some would argue that, because there is still an uncontestable possibility in germline therapy for eliminating, so directly, a slew of threats to our quality of life, we should pursue both germline and somatic therapy. I would not stress this point; mainly because, as opponents of germline therapy state, there are more immediate and important altruistic needs that need to be addressed. For example, using a utilitarian approach to ethics, there currently exists widespread human suffering in the form of poverty and hunger in more individuals than the unfortunate minority who have genetic disorders. With such an unceasing demand for altruism existing throughout the world—requiring insatiable quantities of money, time, and energy—the once exciting possibility of germline therapy becomes an uncertainty that, for the ethical utilitarian, isn't worth the gamble or delay. However, as humans—assuredly not ultimately altruistic beings—we allow in our ethics endeavors that are not strictly altruistic, and I believe that it is

Transhumanists Favor Reaching a Higher Level of Human Achievement

In the case of germ-line enhancements, the potential gains are enormous. Only rarely, however, are the potential gains discussed, perhaps because they are too obvious to be of much theoretical interest. By contrast, uncovering subtle and non-trivial ways in which manipulating our genome could undermine deep values is philosophically a lot more challenging. But if we think about it, we recognize that the promise of genetic enhancements is anything but insignificant. Being free from severe genetic diseases would be good, as would having a mind that can learn more quickly, or having a more robust immune system. Healthier, wittier, happier people may be able to reach new levels culturally. To achieve a significant enhancement of human capacities would be to embark on the transhuman journey of exploration of some of the modes of being that are not accessible to us as we are currently constituted, possibly to discover and to instantiate important new values. On an even more basic level, genetic engineering holds great potential for alleviating unnecessary human suffering. Every day that the introduction of effective human genetic enhancement is delayed is a day of lost individual and cultural potential, and a day of torment for many unfortunate sufferers of diseases that could have been prevented. Seen in this light, proponents of a ban or a moratorium on human genetic modification must take on a heavy burden of proof in order to have the balance of reason tilt in their favor. Transhumanists conclude that the challenge has not been met.

Nick Bostrom, Journal of Value Inquiry, *vol. 37, no. 4, 2003.*

not germline therapy but germline enhancement that holds the incredible promise well worth exploring.

Always Risks When Pushing Humanity Forward

To put a man upon the moon, the government risked the lives of dozens of astronauts, spent billions of dollars that could have easily gone to humanitarian aid—even continuing after the first mission took three lives—and all on a gamble that such a feat was even possible. By most citizens, however, the Apollo missions were considered ethically permissible, even grand, all because it furthered the knowledge and ability of mankind. Armstrong's "giant leap" brought us a little closer to a collective epiphany, a realm of experience once uncharted but now traversed. Although such speech can seem idealistic and, in a strange way, uncaring, this too is a part of man's nature. We obsess over genius, celebrate Columbus for a day despite his cruelty towards the natives, and continue to race, in our professions and passions, towards that ever-illusive goal of further understanding, often at heavy costs. Curiosity and the desire to go beyond lie within the core of human nature; therefore, as it is ethical for a praying mantis to eat her mate, it is ethical for us as humans to continue to follow our impulse onward, accelerating technology and our command over nature and continuing to improve ourselves and our understanding of the world. If the confines of ethics were based entirely around a utilitarian view, it would be unethical to progress in anything but more efficient ways of alleviating pain and suffering. Such a view seems absurd, given human history.

As man has recently triumphed in the discovery of his own genome, researchers from around the globe have been desperate to put the document to use. We have now a rough blueprint of ourselves, but for what? Germline enhancement—one of the proposed methods of genetic engineering—offers perhaps the most profound and teasingly transcendent of all hints. Just as we, throughout history, took nature into our hands, traversing the moon and, shortly, Mars; harnessing the energy from atoms to fuel and destroy our fellow man, we, the citizens of the United States, who empower the most influential government in the world, should surely desire to wield this blueprint of our own creation, and such a desire should not be received with any more fear and disgust than the history that brought us here. At the 1998 Engineering the Human Germline Symposium, [molecular biologist] Lee Silver summarized well this inevitable, human force we must accept:

Countering Naysayers

I think it's important not to make the mistake of thinking that technology is always going to stay the same as it is now. Technology always goes forward. There are radical new technologies that surprise us all the time. And we've got a long time in the future to go. This is my conclusion: Human evolution will be self-driven.

Where we could drive our own evolution with germline enhancement is largely unknown, but current speculation leads us all the way to the fundamental traits that make us human, such as emotional stability, intelligence, [and] the ability to learn.

More contemporary arguments against genetic enhancement (those not based on thousand year-old books) address some important issues. One such argument deals with social repercussions. Under this argument, gene therapy and enhancement would cost thousands of dollars, while many Americans, much less people in poorer countries, can't afford health care. They also predict that this would create class division, which, ethically, is a step in the wrong direction. The Alphas with the better genes would keep to the Alphas, and the Gammas would keep to the poor, genetically unfit, natural Gammas, The argument goes on to theorize that the rich and poor, even more so than normally, would keep, with genetic enhancement, to themselves in preservation of their pure genetic bloodline.

Such an argument has a difficult time justifying its alarmist, reactionary assumptions. Perhaps those who care about keeping to a bloodline will stay within the genetically-altered, but, just as our culture today does not keep to the same races or judge others for their genes, for such a dystopia to occur it would require a massive cultural change. The argument simply places the blame in the wrong place; it blames the amoral tool of genetic enhancement rather than the immoral cultural swing towards deeper class division that would have had to take place. Other arguments against genetic enhancement can be countered in a similar fashion. Some argue that children who are genetically engineered will lose their sense of self and feel predetermined. A similar argument is that those who are engineered for specific purposes will never find their own purpose; they are pigeonholed, the argument claims, from birth by their own parents.

Enhancement Is Not Unethical

In a rebuttal for the former argument, if a person who was genetically engineered feels determined and without a sense of self, he does not properly grasp or believe in genetics. If he did, he would realize that believing in the determining power of genetics means believing in the determination of all life forms, since genes are ubiquitous to life. Simply because genes were consciously decided rather than subconsciously does not mean they are any more determined. For example, in philosophy, neither determinism (every action is caused, or necessitated, by another action) nor indeterminism (actions are either caused or random) is enough to warrant freewill. Likewise, (and I repeat this because it is important) genetic engineering does nothing more than consciously select what we normally would select subconsciously through our natural attraction towards mates. How is it suddenly unethical to want an attractive, smart baby when it is perfectly ethical to desire an attractive, smart mate who will consequently provide that attractive, smart baby ultimately desired?

The argument that it is unethical for parents to predetermine their child's profession and interests, to the point of intolerance towards other interests, I wholeheartedly agree with, though I find it unrelated to the issue of germline enhancement. The connection opponents make is an assumed correlation: bad parents who demand a profession or trait from their child will want to use germline enhancement to secure that trait. The technology of germline enhancement is not to blame for bad parenting; in fact, ironically, in this scenario germline enhancement is ethically positive. The child who is more likely to be what his bad parents want him to be (say, a football player) is more likely to be happy than the child who is not what his parents want (say, a chess player). Any process that could turn chess players into football players would be ethical and beneficial in this situation, since a child is happier having his parents' acceptance.

There is also the medical argument that there cannot be patient consent when utilizing germline enhancement (the child is enhanced along with every proceeding generation but not the deciding adult), therefore it is unethical. This statement seems to contradict with other cultural and even doctoral norms. For instance, I was circumcised, and I do not remember granting consent, and if I could have granted consent, I surely would not have! The idea that consent is needed for a beneficial genetic procedure—a procedure that a previous argument claimed would elevate the rich to dystopian levels—seems absurd.

Moving Forward

Human curiosity and the corresponding rise in scientific understanding, technology, and mastery of nature appears to be a deep-rooted, exponentially growing trend throughout human history. This trend can be shunned or considered immoral, but it is still within us. If, as citizens of the world's current superpower, we decide to accept this trend, to make ethical decisions around this basic drive in a way that contributes to the happiness of mankind, then we must go forth, adventurous yet cautious, and explore before our lifetimes end the most exciting regions of curiosity that remain. Genetic enhancement—consciously controlling our own evolution—promises to be one of the most profound scientific endeavors yet. [As medical thinker and author Gregory Stock states] "We're unraveling our own blueprint and beginning to tinker with it, which is extraordinary." We could turn away, but it is not our nature; though, if we wanted it to, that could someday change.

> *"The vision of one's child as a nearly useless copy of Windows 95 should make parents fight . . . to make sure we never get started down [the genetic enhancement] path."*

The Genetic Enhancement of Children Should Be Opposed

Bill McKibbon

Bill McKibbon is a columnist and the author of Enough: Staying Human in an Engineered Age, *from which the following viewpoint is excerpted. McKibbon argues that parents' desire to improve upon the lives of their children will ensure a market for genetic enhancement of children. Once such modifications are made, however, they will never be comparable to the enhancements available to succeeding generations. In fact, he maintains that engineered children will always be lacking in comparison to others who take advantage of the newest enhancements just a few months or years later. Because this process will "accelerate endlessly and unstoppably," McKibbon insists that genetic enhancement must be prevented from ever beginning.*

As you read, consider the following questions:

1. What is the difference between somatic gene therapy and germline genetic engineering, as McKibbon describes them?

2. What problem does the "arms race" metaphor reveal about genetic manipulation, in the author's view?

3. What examples does McKibbon use to demonstrate that parents already attempt to engineer their children's futures without genetic manipulation?

Right up until [the new millennium], the genes that humans carried in their bodies were exclusively the result of chance—of how the genes of the sperm and the egg, the father and the mother, combined. The only way you could intervene in the process was by choosing who you would mate with—and that was as much wishful thinking as anything else, as generation upon generation of surprised parents have discovered.

But that is changing. We now know two different methods to change human genes. The first, and less controversial, is called somatic gene therapy. Somatic gene therapy begins with an existing individual—someone with, say, cystic fibrosis. Researchers try to deliver new, modified genes to some of her cells, usually by putting the genes aboard viruses they inject into the patient, hoping that the viruses will infect the cells and thereby transmit the genes. Somatic gene therapy is, in other words, much like medicine. You take an existing patient with an existing condition, and you in essence try and convince her cells to manufacture the medicine she needs.

Germline genetic engineering on the other hand is something very novel indeed. "Germ" here refers not to microbes, but to the egg and sperm cells, the germ cells of the human being. Scientists intent on genetic engineering would probably start with a fertilized embryo a week or so old. They would tease apart the cells of that embryo, and then, selecting one, they would add to, delete, or modify some of its genes. They could also insert artificial chromosomes containing prede-signed genes. They would then take the cell, place it inside an egg whose nucleus had been removed, and implant the result-ing new embryo inside a woman. The embryo would, if all went according to plan, grow into a genetically engineered child. His genes would be pushing out proteins to meet the particular choices made by his parents, and by the companies and clinicians they were buying the genes from. Instead of coming solely from the combination of his parents, and thus the combination of their parents, and so on back through time, those genes could come from any other person, or any other plant or animal, or out of the thin blue sky. And once implanted they will pass to his children, and on into time.

The Market for Enhancement Exists

But all this work will require one large change in our current way of doing business. Instead of making babies by making love, we will have to move conception to the laboratory. You need to have the embryo out there where you can work on it—to make the necessary copies, try to add or delete genes, and then implant the one that seems likely to turn out best. Gregory Stock, a researcher at the University of California and an apostle of the new genetic technologies, says that "the union of egg and sperm from two individuals . . . would be too unpredictable with intercourse." And once you've got the embryo out on the lab bench, gravity disappears altogether. "Ultimately," says Michael West, CEO of Advanced Cell Tech-nology, the firm furthest out on the cutting edge of these technologies, "the dream of biologists is to have the sequence of DNA, the programming code of life, and to be able to edit it the way you can a document on a word processor."

Does it sound far-fetched? We began doing it with animals (mice) in 1978, and we've managed the trick with most of the obvious mammals, except one. Some of the first germline in-terventions might be semimedical. You might, say some advocates, start by improving "visual and auditory acuity," first to eliminate nearsightedness or prevent deafness, then to "improve artistic potential." But why stop there? "If something has evolved elsewhere, then it is possible for us to determine its genetic basis and transfer it into the human genome," says Princeton geneticist Lee Silver—just as we have stuck flounder genes into strawberries to keep them from freezing, and jelly-fish genes into rabbits and monkeys to make them glow in the dark.

But would we actually do this? Is there any real need to raise these questions as more than curiosities, or will the schemes simply fade away on their own, ignored by the parents who are their necessary consumers?

Anyone who has entered a baby supply store in the last few years knows that even the soberest parents can be counted on to spend virtually unlimited sums in pursuit of successful offspring. What if the "Baby Einstein" video series, which immerses "learning enabled" babies in English, Spanish, Japanese, Hebrew, German, Russian, and French, could be bolstered with a little gene-tweaking to improve memory? What if the Wombsongs prenatal music system, piping in Brahms to your waiting fetus, could be supplemented with an auditory upgrade? One sociologist told the *New York Times* we'd crossed the line from parenting to "product development," and even if that remark is truer in Manhattan than elsewhere, it's not hard to imagine what such attitudes will mean across the affuent world. . . .

A few of the would-be parents out on the current cutting edge of the reproduction revolution—those who need to obtain sperm or eggs for in vitro fertilization—exhibit similar zeal. Ads started appearing in Ivy League college newspapers a few years ago: couples were willing to pay $50,000 for an egg, provided the donor was at least five feet, ten inches tall, white, and had scored 1400 on her SATs. There is, in other words, a market just waiting for the first clinic with a catalogue of germline modifications. . . .

The Unintended Consequences of Genetic Manipulation

Many geneticists believe that the genetic causality of higher-order behaviors and characteristics like personality, intelligence, or even height is so complex that we will never be able to manipulate it. But this is precisely where the danger lies: we will be constantly tempted to think that we understand this causality better than we really do, and will face even nastier surprises than we did when we tried to conquer the non-human natural environment. In this case, the victim of a failed experiment will not be an ecosystem, but a human child whose parents, seeking to give her greater intelligence, will saddle her with a greater propensity for cancer, or prolonged debility in old age, or some other completely unexpected side effect that may emerge only after the experimenters have passed from the scene.

Francis Fukuyana, World Watch, *July/August 2002.*

Being Left Behind in the Arms Race

But say you're not ready. Say you're perfectly happy with the prospect of a child who shares the unmodified genes of you and your partner. Say you think that manipulating the DNA of your child might be dangerous, or presumptuous, or icky? How long will you be able to hold that line if the procedure begins to spread among your neighbors? Maybe not so long as you think: if germline manipulation actually does begin, it seems likely to set off a kind of biological arms race. "Suppose parents could add thirty points to their child's IQ," asks MIT [Massachusetts Institute of Technology] economist Lester Thurow. "Wouldn't you want to do it? And if you don't, your child will be the stupidest in the neighborhood." That's precisely what it might feel like to be the parent facing the choice.

Individual competition more or less defines the society we've built, and in that context love can almost be defined as giving your kids what they need to make their way in the world. Deciding not to soup them up ... well, it could come to seem like child abuse.

Of course, the problem about arms races is that you never really get anywhere. If everyone's adding thirty IQ points, then having an IQ of one hundred fifty won't get you any closer to Stanford than you were at the outset. The very first athlete engineered to use twice as much oxygen as the next guy will be unbeatable in the Tour de France—but in no time he'll merely be the new standard. You'll have to do what he did to be in the race, but your upgrades won't put you ahead, merely back on a level playing field. You might be able to argue that society as a whole was helped, because there was more total brainpower at work, but your kid won't be any closer to the top of the pack. All you'll be able to do is guarantee she won't be left hopelessly far behind.

In fact, the arms-race problem has an extra ironic twist when it comes to genetic manipulation. The United States and the Soviet Union could, and did, keep adding new weapons to their arsenals over the decades. But with germline manipulation, you get only one shot; the extra chromosome you stick in your kid when he's born is the one he carries throughout his life. So let's say baby Sophie has a state-of-the-art gene job: her parents paid for the proteins discovered by, say, 2005 that, on average, yielded ten extra IQ points. By the time Sophie is five, though, scientists will doubtless have discovered ten more genes linked to intelligence. Now anyone with a platinum card can get twenty IQ points, not to mention a memory boost and a permanent wrinkle-free brow. So by the time Sophie is twenty-five and in the job market, she's already more or less obsolete—the kids coming out of college just plain have better hardware.

"For all his billions, [Microsoft cofounder] Bill Gates could not have purchased a single genetic enhancement for his son Rory John," writes Gregory Stock, at the University of California. "And you can bet that any enhancements a billion dollars can buy Rory's child in 2030 will seem crude alongside those available for modest sums in 2060." It's not, he adds, "so different from upgraded software. You'll want the new release."

Existing Engineering

The vision of one's child as a nearly useless copy of Windows 95 should make parents fight like hell to make sure we never get started down this path. But the vision gets lost easily in the gushing excitement about "improving" the opportunities for our kids. . . .

We already "engineer" our offspring in some sense of the word: we do our best, and often our worst, to steer them in particular directions. And our worst can be pretty bad. We all know people whose lives were blighted trying to meet the expectations of their parents. We've all seen the crazed devotion to getting kids into the right schools, the right professions, the right income brackets. Parents try and pass down their prejudices, their politics, their attitude toward the world ("we've got to toughen that kid up—he's going to get walked all over"). . . .

We try and shape the lives of our kids—to "improve" their lives, as we would measure improvement—but our gravity is usually weak enough that kids can break out of it if and when they need to. (When it isn't, when parents manage to bend their children to the point of breaking, we think of them as monstrous.) "Many of the most creative and valuable human lives are the result of particularly diffcult struggles" against expectation and influence, writes the legal scholar Martha Nussbaum.

That's not how a genetic engineer thinks of his product. . . . "With reprogenetics," writes Lee Silver, "parents can gain complete control over their destiny, with the ability to guide and enhance the characteristics of their children, and their children's children as well." Such parents would not be calling their children on the phone at annoyingly frequent intervals to suggest that it's time to get a real job; instead, . . . they would be inserting genes that produced proteins that would make their child behave in certain ways throughout his life. You cannot rebel against the production of that protein. Perhaps you can still do everything in your power to defeat the wishes of your parents, but that protein will nonetheless be pumped out relentlessly into your system, defining who you are. . . .

There Is Still Time to Save Humanity

Right now both the genes, and the limits that they set on us, connect us with every human that came before. Human beings can look at rock art carved into African cliffs and French caves thirty thousand years ago and feel an electric, immediate kinship. We've gone from digging sticks to combines, and from drum circles to symphony orchestras (and back again to drum circles), but we still hear in the same range and see in the same spectrum, still produce adrenaline and dopamine in the same ways, still think in many of the same patterns. We are, by and large, the same people, more closely genetically related to one another than we may be to our engineered grandchildren.

These new technologies show us that human meaning dangles by a far thinner thread than we had thought. If germline genetic engineering ever starts, it will accelerate endlessly and unstoppably into the future, as individuals make the calculation that they have no choice but to equip their kids for the world that's being made. The first child whose genes come in part from some corporate lab, the first child who has been "enhanced" from what came before—that's the first child who will glance back over his shoulder and see a gap between himself and human history. . . .

These new technologies, however, are not yet inevitable. Unlike global warming, this genie is not yet out of the bottle. But if germline genetic engineering is going to be stopped, it will have to happen now, before it's quite begun. It will have to be a political choice—that is, one we make not as parents but as citizens, not as individuals but as a whole, thinking not only about our own offspring but about everyone.

So far the discussion has been confined to a few scientists, a few philosophers, a few ideologues. It needs to spread widely, and quickly, and loudly. The stakes are absurdly high, nothing less than the meaning of being human. And given the seductions that we've seen—the intuitively and culturally delicious prospect of a better child—the arguments against must be not only powerful but also deep. They'll need to resonate on the same intuitive and cultural level. We'll need to feel in our gut the reasons why, this time, we should tell Prometheus thanks, but no thanks.

| "*[Coming] technological revolutions will allow us to transcend our frail bodies with all their limitations.*"

Future Technology Will Benignly Alter Human Existence

Ray Kurzweil

In the following viewpoint, Ray Kurzweil predicts that trends in technology will eventually change humanity. According to Kurzweil, genetic advancements will defeat disease and allow people to live longer; nanotechnology will restructure machinery and biology; and robotics will breed wondrous artificial intelligence that will merge with and improve human understanding. In time, a human-machine civilization will arise in which poverty, pollution, hunger, disease and other concerns will be overcome and the powers of thought and communication will be exponentially increased beyond what is currently imaginable. Ray Kurzweil is an inventor, scientist, author, and futurist.

As you read, consider the following questions:

1. As Kurzweil describes it, what is the "Singularity"?

2. How does the author envision the use of nanotechnology in benefiting medical treatment?

3. In Kurzweil's view, why will artificial intelligence necessarily exceed human intelligence?

We stand on the threshold of the most profound and transformative event in the history of humanity, the "Singularity."

What is the Singularity? From my perspective, the Singularity is a future period during which the pace of technological change will be so fast and far-reaching that human existence on this planet will be irreversibly altered. We will combine our brain power—the knowledge, skills, and personality quirks that make us human—with our computer power in order to think, reason, communicate, and create in ways we can scarcely even contemplate today.

This merger of man and machine, coupled with the sudden explosion in machine intelligence and rapid innovation in the fields of gene research as well as nanotechnology, will result in a world where there is no distinction between the biological and the mechanical, or between physical and virtual reality. These technological revolutions will allow us to transcend our frail bodies with all their limitations. Illness, as we know it, will be eradicated. Through the use of nanotechnology, we will be able to manufacture almost any physical product upon demand, world hunger and poverty will be solved, and pollution will vanish. Human existence will undergo a quantum leap in evolution. We will be able to live as long as we choose. The coming into being of such a world is, in essence, the Singularity.

How is it possible we could be so close to this enormous change and not see it? The answer is the quickening nature of technological innovation. In thinking about the future, few people take into consideration the fact that human scientific progress is exponential: It expands by repeatedly multiplying by a constant (10 times 10 times 10 and so on) rather than linear; that is, expanding by repeatedly adding a constant (10 plus 10 plus 10, and so on). I emphasize the exponential-versus-linear perspective because it's the most important failure that prognosticators make in considering future trends.

Moving Faster Toward a New World

Our forebears expected what lay ahead of them to resemble what they had already experienced, with few exceptions. Because they lived during a time when the rate of technological innovation was so slow as to be unnoticeable, their expectations of an unchanged future were continually fulfilled. Today, we have witnessed the acceleration of the curve. Therefore, we anticipate continuous technological progress and the social repercussions that follow. We see the future as being different from the present. But the future will be far more surprising than most people realize, because few observers have truly internalized the implications of the fact that the rate of change is itself accelerating.

Exponential growth starts out slowly and virtually unnoticeably, but beyond the knee of the curve it turns explosive and profoundly transformative. My models show that we are doubling the paradigm-shift rate for technology innovation every decade. In other words, the twentieth century was gradually speeding up to today's rate of progress; its achievements, therefore, were equivalent to about 20 years of progress at the rate of 2000. We'll make another "20 years" of progress in just 14 years (by 2014), and then do the same again in only seven years. To express this another way, we won't experience 100 years of technological advance in the twenty-first century; we will witness on the order of 20,000 years of progress (again, when measured by today's progress rate), or progress on a level of about 1,000 times greater than what was achieved in the twentieth century.

How Will We Know the Singularity Is upon Us?

The first half of the twenty-first century will be characterized by three overlapping revolutions—in genetics, nanotechnology, and robotics. These will usher in the beginning of this period of tremendous change I refer to as the Singularity. We are in the early stages of the genetics revolution today. By understanding the information processes underlying life, we are learning to reprogram our biology to achieve the virtual elimination of disease, dramatic expansion of human potential, and radical life extension. However, Hans Moravec of Carnegie Mellon University's Robotics Institute points out that no matter how successfully we fine-tune our DNA-based biology, biology will never be able to match what we will be able to engineer once we fully understand life's principles of operation. In other words, we will always be "second-class robots."

The nanotechnology revolution will enable us to redesign and rebuild—molecule by molecule—our bodies and brains and the world with which we interact, going far beyond the limitations of biology.

But the most powerful impending revolution is the robotic revolution. By robotic, I am not referring exclusively—or even primarily—to humanoid-looking droids that take up physical space, but rather to artificial intelligence in all its variations.

Following, I have laid out the principal components underlying each of these coming technological revolutions. While each new wave of progress will solve the problems from earlier transformations, each will also introduce new perils, but each, operating both separately and in concert, underpins the Singularity.

The Genetic Revolution

Genetic and molecular science will extend biology and correct its obvious flaws (such as our vulnerability to disease). By the year 2020, the full effects of the genetic revolution will be felt across society. We are rapidly gaining the knowledge and the tools to drastically extend the usability of the "house" each of us calls his body and brain.

Nanomedicine researcher Robert Freitas estimates that eliminating 50% of medically preventable conditions would extend human life expectancy 150 years. If we were able to prevent 90% of naturally occurring medical problems, we'd live to be more than 1,000 years old.

We can see the beginnings of this awesome medical revolution today. The field of genetic biotechnology is fueled by the growing arsenal of tools. Drug discovery was once a matter of finding substrates (chemicals) that produced some beneficial result without excessive side effects, a research method similar to early humans' seeking out rocks and other natural implements that could be used for helpful purposes. Today we are discovering the precise biochemical pathways that underlie both disease and aging processes. We are able to design drugs to carry out precise missions at the molecular level. With recently developed gene technologies, we're on the verge of being able to control how genes express themselves. Gene expression is the process by which cellular components (specifically RNA and the ribosomes) produce proteins according to a precise genetic blueprint. While every human cell contains a complete DNA sample, and thus the full complement of the body's genes, a specific cell, such as a skin cell or a pancreatic islet cell, gets its characteristics from only the fraction of genetic information relevant to that particular cell type.

Gene expression is controlled by peptides (molecules made up of sequences of up to 100 amino acids) and short RNA strands. We are now beginning to learn how these processes work. Many new therapies currently in development and testing are based on manipulating peptides either to turn off the expression of disease-causing genes or to turn on desirable genes that may otherwise not be expressed in a particular type of cell. A new technique called RNA interference is able to destroy the messenger RNA expressing a gene and thereby effectively turn that gene off.

Accelerating progress in biotechnology will enable us to reprogram our genes and metabolic processes to propel the fields of genomics (influencing genes), proteomics (understanding and influencing the role of proteins), gene therapy (suppressing gene expression as well as adding new genetic information), rational drug design (formulating drugs that target precise changes in disease and aging processes), as well as the therapeutic cloning of rejuvenated cells, tissues, and organs.

The Nanotechnology Revolution

Nanotechnology promises the tools to rebuild the physical world—our bodies and brains included—molecular fragment by molecular fragment and potentially atom by atom. We are shrinking the key features (working parts), in accordance with the law of accelerating returns, at an exponential rate (over four per linear dimension per decade or about 100 per 3-D volume). At this rate the key feature sizes for most electronic and many mechanical technologies will be in the nanotechnology range—generally considered to be less than 100 nanometers (one billionth of one meter)—by the 2020s. Electronics has already dipped below this threshold, although not yet in three-dimensional structures and not yet in structures that are capable of assembling other similar structures—an essential step before nanotechnology can reach its promised potential. Meanwhile, rapid progress has been made recently in preparing the conceptual framework and design ideas for the coming age of nanotechnology.

Nanotechnology has expanded to include any technology in which a machine's key features are measured by fewer than 100 nanometers. Just as contemporary electronics has already quietly slipped into this nano realm, the area of biological and medical applications has already entered the era of nanoparticles, in which nanoscale objects are being developed to create more-effective tests and treatments.

In the area of testing and diagnosis, nanoparticles are already being employed in experimental biological tests as tags and labels to greatly enhance sensitivity in detecting substances such as proteins. Magnetic nanotags can be used to bind with antibodies that can then be read using magnetic probes while still inside the body. Successful experiments have been conducted with gold nanoparticles that are bound to DNA segments and can rapidly test for specific DNA sequences in a sample. Small nanoscale beads called quantum dots can be programmed with specific codes combining multiple colors, similar to a color bar code, that can facilitate tracking of substances through the body.

In the future, nanoscale devices will run hundreds of tests simultaneously on tiny samples of a given substance. These devices will allow extensive tests to be conducted on nearly invisible samples of blood.

In the area of treatment, a particularly exciting application of this technology is the harnessing of nanoparticles to deliver medication to specific sites in the body. Nanoparticles can guide drugs into cell walls and through the blood-brain barrier. Nanoscale packages can be designed to hold drugs, protect them through the gastrointestinal tract, ferry them to specific locations, and then release them in sophisticated ways that can be influenced and controlled, wirelessly, from outside the body.

Nanotherapeutics in Alachua, Florida, has developed a biodegradable polymer only several nanometers thick that uses this approach. Meanwhile, scientists at McGill University in Montreal have demonstrated a nanopill with structures in the 25 to 45 nanometer range. The nanopill is small enough to pass through the cell wall and deliver medications directly to targeted structures inside the cell.

MicroCHIPS of Bedford, Massachusetts, has developed a computerized device that is implanted under the skin and delivers precise mixtures of medicines from hundreds of nanoscale wells inside the device. Future versions of the device are expected to be able to measure blood levels of substances such as glucose. The system could be used as an artificial pancreas, releasing precise amounts of insulin based on the blood glucose response. The system would also be capable of simulating any other hormone-producing organ, and if trials go smoothly, the system could be on the market by 2008. Another innovative proposal is to guide nanoparticles (probably composed of gold) to a tumor site and then heat them with infrared beams to destroy the cancer cells.

The revolution in nanotechnology will allow us to do a great deal more than simply treat disease. Ultimately, nanotech will enable us to redesign and rebuild not only our bodies and brains, but also the world with which we interact. The full realization of nanotechnology, however, will lag behind the biotechnology revolution by about one decade. But by the mid to late 2020s, the effects of the nanotech revolution will be widespread and obvious.

Nanotechnology and the Human Brain

The most important and radical application particularly of circa-2030 nanobots will be to expand our minds through the merger of biological and nonbiological, or "machine," intelligence. In the next 25 years, we will learn how to augment our 100 trillion very slow interneuronal connections with high-speed virtual connections via nanorobotics. This will allow us to greatly boost our pattern-recognition abilities, memories, and overall thinking capacity, as well as to directly interface with powerful forms of computer intelligence. The technology will also provide wireless communication from one brain to another.

Humans, the Lower Life Form

In the future, I believe, we will be able to send signals to and from human and machine brains. We will be able to directly harness the memory and mathematical capabilities of machines. We will be able to communicate across the internet by means of thought signals alone. Human speech and language, as we know it, will become obsolete. Ultimately, humans will become a lower form of life, unable to compete with either intelligent machines or cyborgs.

Kevin Warwick, Guardian *(UK), January 26, 2000.*

In other words, the age of telepathic communication is almost upon us.

Our brains today are relatively fixed in design. Although we do add patterns of interneuronal connections and neurotransmitter concentrations as a normal part of the learning process, the current overall capacity of the human brain is highly constrained. As humanity's artificial-intelligence (AI) capabilities begin to upstage our human intelligence at the end of the 2030s, we will be able to move beyond the basic architecture of the brain's neural regions.

Brain implants based on massively distributed intelligent nanobots will greatly expand our memories and otherwise vastly improve all of our sensory, pattern-recognition, and cognitive abilities. Since the nanobots will be communicating with one another, they will be able to create any set of new neural connections, break existing connections (by suppressing neural firing), create new hybrid biological and computer networks, and add completely mechanical networks, as well as interface intimately with new computer programs and artificial intelligences.

The implementation of artificial intelligence in our biological systems will mark an evolutionary leap forward for humanity, but it also implies we will indeed become more "machine" than "human." Billions of nanobots will travel through the bloodstream in our bodies and brains. In our bodies, they will destroy pathogens, correct DNA errors, eliminate toxins, and perform many other tasks to enhance our physical well-being. As a result, we will be able to live indefinitely without aging.

In our brains, nanobots will interact with our biological neurons. This will provide full-immersion virtual reality incorporating all of the senses, as well as neurological correlates of our emotions, from within the nervous system. More importantly, this intimate connection between our biological thinking and the machine intelligence we are creating will profoundly expand human intelligence.

Warfare will move toward nanobot-based weapons, as well as cyber-weapons. Learning will first move online, but once our brains are fully online we will be able to download new knowledge and skills. The role of work will be to create knowledge of all kinds, from music and art to math and science. The role of play will also be to create knowledge. In the future, there won't be a clear distinction between work and play.

The Robotic Revolution

Of the three technological revolutions underlying the Singularity (genetic, nano-mechanical, and robotic), the most profound is robotic or, as it is commonly called, the *strong artificial intelligence* revolution. This refers to the creation of computer thinking ability that exceeds the thinking ability of humans. We are very close to the day when fully biological humans (as we now know them today) cease to be the dominant intelligence on the planet. By the end of this century, computational or mechanical intelligence will be trillions of trillions of times more powerful than unaided human brain power. I argue that computer, or as I call it *nonbiological intelligence*, should still be considered human since it is fully derived from human-machine civilization and will be based, at least in part, on a human-made version of a fully functional human brain. The merger of these two worlds of intelligence is not merely a merger of biological and mechanical thinking mediums, but also and more importantly, a merger of method and organizational thinking that will expand our minds in virtually every imaginable way.

Biological human thinking is limited to 10 to the 16th power calculations per second (cps) per human brain (based on neuromorphic modeling of brain regions) and about 10 to the 26th power cps for all human brains. These figures will not appreciably change, even with bioengineering adjustments to our genome. The processing capacity of nonbiological intelligence or strong AI, in contrast, is growing at an exponential rate (with the rate itself increasing) and will vastly exceed biological intelligence by the mid-2040s.

Artificial intelligence will necessarily exceed human intelligence for several reasons.

First, machines can share knowledge and communicate with one another far more efficiently than can humans. As humans, we do not have the means to exchange the vast patterns of interneuronal connections and neurotransmitter-concentration levels that comprise our learning, knowledge, and skills, other than through slow, language-based communication.

Second, humanity's intellectual skills have developed in ways that have been evolutionarily encouraged in natural environments. Those skills, which are primarily based on our abilities to recognize and extract meaning from patterns, enable us to be highly proficient in certain tasks such as distinguishing faces, identifying objects, and recognizing language sounds. Unfortunately, our brains are less well-suited for dealing with more-complex patterns, such as those that exist in financial, scientific, or product data. The application of computer-based techniques will allow us to fully master pattern-recognition paradigms. Finally, as human knowledge migrates to the Web, machines will demonstrate increased proficiency in reading, understanding, and synthesizing all human-machine information.

The Chicken or the Egg?

A key question regarding the Singularity is whether the "chicken" (strong AI) or the "egg" (nanotechnology) will come first. In other words, will strong AI lead to full nanotechnology (molecular-manufacturing assemblers that can turn information into physical products), or will full nanotechnology lead to strong AI?

The logic of the first premise is that strong AI would be in a position to solve any remaining design problems required to implement full nanotechnology. The second premise is based on the assumption that hardware requirements for strong AI will be met by nanotechnology-based computation. Likewise, the software requirements for engineering strong AI would be facilitated by nanobots. These microscopic machines will allow us to create highly detailed scans of human brains along with diagrams of how the human brain is able to do all the wonderful things that have long mystified us, such as create meaning, contextualize information, and experience emotion. Once we fully understand how the brain functions, we will be able to re-create the phenomena of human thinking in machines. We will endow computers, already superior to us in the performance of mechanical tasks, with lifelike intelligence.

Progress in both areas (nano and robotic) will necessarily use our most-advanced tools, so advances in each field will simultaneously facilitate the other. However, I do expect that the most important nanotechnological breakthroughs will emerge prior to strong AI, but only by a few years (around 2025 for nanotechnology and 2029 for strong AI).

As revolutionary as nanotechnology will be, strong AI will have far more profound consequences. Nanotechnology is powerful but not necessarily intelligent. We can devise ways of at least trying to manage the enormous powers of nanotechnology, but superintelligence by its nature cannot be controlled.

The nano/robotic revolution will also force us to reconsider the very definition of *human*. Not only will we be surrounded by machines that will display distinctly human characteristics, but we will be less human from a literal standpoint.

Despite the wonderful future potential of medicine, real human longevity will only be attained when we move away from our biological bodies entirely. As we move toward a software-based existence, we will gain the means of "backing ourselves up" (storing the key patterns underlying our knowledge, skills, and personality in a digital setting) thereby enabling a virtual immortality. Thanks to nanotechnology, we will have bodies that we can not just modify but change into new forms at will. We will be able to quickly change our bodies in full-immersion virtual-reality environments incorporating all of the senses during the 2020s and in *real* reality in the 2040s.

Implications of the Singularity

What will be the nature of human experience once computer intelligence predominates? What are the implications for the human-machine civilization when strong AI and nanotechnology can create any product, any situation, any environment that we can imagine at will? I stress the role of imagination here because we will still be constrained in our creations to what we can imagine. But our tools for bringing imagination to life are growing exponentially more powerful.

People often go through three stages in considering the impact of future technology: awe and wonderment at its potential to overcome age-old problems, then a sense of dread at the new grave dangers that accompany these novel technologies, followed finally by the realization that the only viable and responsible path is to set a careful course that can realize the benefits while managing the dangers.

My own expectation is that the creative and constructive applications of these technologies will dominate, as I believe they do today. However, we need to vastly increase our investment in developing specific defensive technologies. We are at the critical stage where we need to directly implement defensive technologies for nanotechnology during the late teen years of this century.

I believe that a narrow relinquishment of the development of certain capabilities needs to be part of our ethical response to the dangers of twenty-first-century technological challenges. For example, [cofounder of Sun Microsystems and future tech centre] Bill Joy and I wrote a joint op-ed piece in the *New York Times* criticizing the publication of the 1918 flu genome on the web as it constitutes a dangerous blueprint. Another constructive example of this is the ethical guidelines proposed by the Foresight Institute: namely, that nanotechnologists agree to relinquish the development of physical entities that can self-replicate in a natural environment free of any human control or override mechanism. However, deciding in favor of too many limitations and restrictions would undermine economic progress and is ethically unjustified given the opportunity to alleviate disease, overcome poverty, and clean up the environment.

We don't have to look past today to see the intertwined promise and peril of technological advancement. Imagine describing the dangers (atomic and hydrogen bombs for one thing) that exist today to people who lived a couple of hundred years ago. They would think it mad to take such risks. But how many people in 2006 would really want to go back to the short, brutish, disease-filled, poverty-stricken, disaster-prone lives that 99% of the human race struggled through two centuries ago?

We may romanticize the past, but up until fairly recently most of humanity lived extremely fragile lives in which one all-too-common misfortune could spell disaster. Two hundred years ago, life expectancy for females in the record-holding country (Sweden) was roughly 35 years, very brief compared with the longest life expectancy today—almost 85 years for Japanese women. Life expectancy for males was roughly 33 years, compared with the current 79 years. Half a day was often required to prepare an evening meal, and hard labor characterized most human activity. There were no social safety nets. Substantial portions of our species still live in this precarious way, which is at least one reason to continue technological progress and the economic improvement that accompanies it. Only technology, with its ability to provide orders of magnitude of advances in capability and affordability has the scale to confront problems such as poverty, disease, pollution, and the other overriding concerns of society today. The benefits of applying ourselves to these challenges cannot be overstated.

A New Evolution

As the Singularity approaches, we will have to reconsider our ideas about the nature of human life and redesign our human institutions. Intelligence on and around Earth will continue to expand exponentially until we reach the limits of matter and energy to support intelligent computation. As we approach this limit in our corner of the galaxy, the intelligence of our civilization will expand outward into the rest of the universe, quickly reaching the fastest speed possible. We understand that speed to be the speed of light, but there are suggestions that we may be able to circumvent this apparent limit (conceivably by taking shortcuts through "wormholes," or hypothetical shortcuts through space and time).

A common view is that science has consistently been correcting our overly inflated view of our own significance. [Evolutionary biologist] Stephen Jay Gould said, "The most important scientific revolutions all include, as their only common feature, the dethronement of human arrogance from one pedestal after another of previous convictions about our centrality in the cosmos."

Instead, it turns out we are central. Our ability to create models, virtual realities—in our brains, combined with our modest-looking thumbs, has been sufficient to usher in another form of evolution: technology. That development enabled the persistence of the accelerating pace that started with biological evolution. It will continue until the entire universe is at our fingertips.

Future Technology Could Threaten Human Existence

Bill Joy

Bill Joy is a cofounder of Sun Microsystems. He remained the company's chief scientist until 2003. In that year he helped form HighBar Ventures, a venture capital firm. In the following viewpoint, Joy worries that advances in genetic, robotics, and nanotechnology could prove detrimental to human existence. Chief among his fears is that the self-replicating technology in all of these fields could create legions of uncontrolled beings (clones, robots, or nanobots) that would swamp human life. Furthermore, in Joy's view, more and more people in the Information Age will have access to the knowledge to make this devastation possible, and even an unwitting scientist could start a chain of events that would lead inevitably to the end of humanity.

As you read, consider the following questions:

1. How soon, in Joy's view, could an intelligent robot be built?

2. As the author describes it, what is gray goo and what is its threat to humanity?

3. In outlining the views of other thinkers, what does Joy say are three possible methods of avoiding human extinction in the face of overwhelming technology?

Accustomed to living with almost routine scientific breakthroughs, we have yet to come to terms with the fact that the most compelling 21st-century technologies—robotics, genetic engineering, and nanotechnology—pose a different threat than the technologies that have come before. Specifically, robots, engineered organisms, and nanobots share a dangerous amplifying factor: They can self-replicate. A bomb is blown up only once—but one bot can become many, and quickly get out of control. . . .

What was different in the 20th century? Certainly, the technologies underlying the weapons of mass destruction (WMD)—nuclear, biological, and chemical (NBC)—were powerful, and the weapons an enormous threat. But building nuclear weapons required, at least for a time, access to both rare—indeed, effectively unavailable—raw materials and highly protected information; biological and chemical weapons programs also tended to require large-scale activities.

The 21st-century technologies—genetics, nanotechnology, and robotics (GNR)—are so powerful that they can spawn whole new classes of accidents and abuses. Most dangerously, for the first time, these accidents and abuses are widely within the reach of individuals or small groups. They will not require large facilities or rare raw materials. Knowledge alone will enable the use of them.

Thus we have the possibility not just of weapons of mass destruction but of knowledge-enabled mass destruction (KMD), this destructiveness hugely amplified by the power of self-replication.

I think it is no exaggeration to say we are on the cusp of the further perfection of extreme evil, an evil whose possibility spreads well beyond that which weapons of mass destruction bequeathed to the nation-states, on to a surprising and terrible empowerment of extreme individuals. . . .

Working from Within

Perhaps it is always hard to see the bigger impact while you are in the vortex of a change. Failing to understand the consequences of our inventions while we are in the rapture of discovery and innovation seems to be a common fault of scientists and technologists; we have long been driven by the overarching desire to know that is the nature of science's quest, not stopping to notice that the progress to newer and more powerful technologies can take on a life of its own. . . .

In my own work, as codesigner of three microprocessor architectures—SPARC, picoJava, and MAJC—and as the designer of several implementations thereof, I've been afforded a deep and firsthand acquaintance with Moore's law.[1] For decades, Moore's law has correctly predicted the exponential rate of improvement of semiconductor technology. Until [1999] I believed that the rate of advances predicted by Moore's law might continue only until roughly 2010, when some physical limits would begin to be reached. It was not obvious to me that a new technology would arrive in time to keep performance advancing smoothly.

1. Intel Corporation's cofounder Gordon Moore hypothesized in 1965 that the number of transistors on an integrated circuit doubled every two years. Some observers have extrapolated this to suggest that computing power per unit cost follows suit.

But because of the recent rapid and radical progress in molecular electronics—where individual atoms and molecules replace lithographically drawn transistors—and related nanoscale technologies, we should be able to meet or exceed the Moore's law rate of progress for another 30 years. By 2030, we are likely to be able to build machines, in quantity, a million times as powerful as the personal computers of today . . .

As this enormous computing power is combined with the manipulative advances of the physical sciences and the new, deep understandings in genetics, enormous transformative power is being unleashed. These combinations open up the opportunity to completely redesign the world, for better or worse: The replicating and evolving processes that have been confined to the natural world are about to become realms of human endeavor.

In designing software and microprocessors, I have never had the feeling that I was designing an intelligent machine. The software and hardware is so fragile and the capabilities of the machine to "think" so clearly absent that, even as a possibility, this has always seemed very far in the future.

But now, with the prospect of human-level computing power in about 30 years, a new idea suggests itself: that I may be working to create tools which will enable the construction of the technology that may replace our species. How do I feel about this? Very uncomfortable. Having struggled my entire career to build reliable software systems, it seems to me more than likely that this future will not work out as well as some people may imagine. My personal experience suggests we tend to overestimate our design abilities.

Given the incredible power of these new technologies, shouldn't we be asking how we can best coexist with them? And if our own extinction is a likely, or even possible, outcome of our technological development, shouldn't we proceed with great caution?

Robotic Replacement of Humans

The dream of robotics is, first, that intelligent machines can do our work for us, allowing us lives of leisure, restoring us to Eden. Yet in his history of such ideas, *Darwin among the Machines*, George Dyson warns: "In the game of life and evolution there are three players at the table: human beings, nature, and machines. I am firmly on the side of nature. But nature, I suspect, is on the side of the machines. . . ." [Leading robotics researcher Hans] Moravec agrees, believing we may well not survive the encounter with the superior robot species.

How soon could such an intelligent robot be built? The coming advances in computing power seem to make it possible by 2030. And once an intelligent robot exists, it is only a small step to a robot species—to an intelligent robot that can make evolved copies of itself.

A second dream of robotics is that we will gradually replace ourselves with our robotic technology, achieving near immortality by downloading our consciousnesses; it is this process that [cofounder of Thinking Machines Corporation] Danny Hillis thinks we will gradually get used to and that [inventor and technology prophet] Ray Kurzweil elegantly details in *The Age of Spiritual Machines.* . . .

The Challenge of Genetic Manipulation

But if we are downloaded into our technology, what are the chances that we will thereafter be ourselves or even human? It seems to me far more likely that a robotic existence would not be like a human one in any sense that we understand, that the robots would in no sense be our children, that on this path our humanity may well be lost.

Genetic engineering promises to revolutionize agriculture by increasing crop yields while reducing the use of pesticides; to create tens of thousands of novel species of bacteria, plants, viruses, and animals; to replace reproduction, or supplement it, with cloning; to create cures for many diseases, increasing our life span and our quality of life; and much, much more. We now know with certainty that these profound changes in the biological sciences are imminent and will challenge all our notions of what life is.

Technologies such as human cloning have in particular raised our awareness of the profound ethical and moral issues we face. If, for example, we were to reengineer ourselves into several separate and unequal species using the power of genetic engineering, then we would threaten the notion of equality that is the very cornerstone of our democracy. . . .

Awareness of the dangers inherent in genetic engineering is beginning to grow. . . . The general public is aware of, and uneasy about, genetically modified foods, and seems to be rejecting the notion that such foods should be permitted to be unlabeled.

But genetic engineering technology is already very far along. . . . The USDA [U.S. Department of Agriculture] has already approved about 50 genetically engineered crops for unlimited release; more than half of the world's soybeans and a third of its corn now contain genes spliced in from other forms of life.

While there are many important issues here, my own major concern with genetic engineering is narrower: that it gives the power—whether militarily, accidentally, or in a deliberate terrorist act—to create a White Plague [a man-made plague that kills selectively, from Frank Herbert's science fiction novel of the same name].

The Danger of Destructive Nanotechnology

The many wonders of nanotechnology were first imagined by the Nobel-laureate physicist Richard Feynman in a speech he gave in 1959, subsequently published under the title "There's Plenty of Room at the Bottom." The book that made a big impression on me, in the mid-'80s, was Eric Drexler's *Engines of Creation*, in which he described beautifully how manipulation of matter at the atomic level could create a utopian future of abundance, where just about everything could be made cheaply, and almost any imaginable disease or physical problem could be solved using nanotechnology and artificial intelligences.

A subsequent book, *Unbounding the Future: The Nanotechnology Revolution*, which Drexler cowrote, imagines some of the changes that might take place in a world where we had molecular-level "assemblers." Assemblers could make possible incredibly low-cost solar power, cures for cancer and the common cold by augmentation of the human immune system, essentially complete cleanup of the environment, incredibly inexpensive pocket supercomputers—in fact, any product would be manufacturable by assemblers at a cost no greater than that of wood—spaceflight more accessible than transoceanic travel today, and restoration of extinct species.

I remember feeling good about nanotechnology after reading *Engines of Creation*. As a technologist, it gave me a sense of calm—that is, nanotechnology showed us that incredible progress was possible, and indeed perhaps inevitable. If nanotechnology was our future, then I didn't feel pressed to solve so many problems in the present. I would get to Drexler's utopian future in due time; I might as well enjoy life more in the here and now. It didn't make sense, given his vision, to stay up all night, all the time. . . .

With these wonders came clear dangers, of which I was acutely aware. As I said at a nanotechnology conference in 1989, "We can't simply do our science and not worry about these ethical issues." But my subsequent conversations with physicists convinced me that nanotechnology might not even work—or, at least, it wouldn't work anytime soon. . . .

Then, [in 1999], [physicist] Brosl Hasslacher told me that nanoscale molecular electronics was now practical. This was *new* news, at least to me, and I think to many people—and it radically changed my opinion about nanotechnology. It sent me back to *Engines of Creation*. Rereading Drexler's work after more than 10 years, I was dismayed to realize how little I had remembered of its lengthy section called "Dangers and Hopes," including a discussion of how nanotechnologies can become "engines of destruction." Indeed, in my rereading of this cautionary material today, I am struck by how naive some of Drexler's safeguard proposals seem, and how much greater I judge the dangers to be now than even he seemed to then. . . .

The enabling breakthrough to assemblers seems quite likely within the next 20 years. Molecular electronics—the new subfield of nanotechnology where individual molecules are circuit elements—should mature quickly and become enormously lucrative within this decade, causing a large incremental investment in all nanotechnologies.

Unfortunately, as with nuclear technology, it is far easier to create destructive uses for nanotechnology than constructive ones. Nanotechnology has clear military and terrorist uses, and you need not be suicidal to release a massively destructive nanotechnological device—such devices can be built to be selectively destructive, affecting, for example, only a certain geographical area or a group of people who are genetically distinct.

Gray Goo

An immediate consequence of the Faustian bargain in obtaining the great power of nanotechnology is that we run a grave risk—the risk that we might destroy the biosphere on which all life depends.

As Drexler explained:

"Plants" with "leaves" no more efficient than today's solar cells could out-compete real plants, crowding the biosphere with an inedible foliage. Tough omnivorous "bacteria" could out-compete real bacteria: They could spread like blowing pollen, replicate swiftly, and reduce the biosphere to dust in a

Only One, Narrow Vision of the Future

We must . . . refine and enlarge our understanding of what constitutes *human progress*. When the extinctionists [i.e., those who glumly predict the end of humanity in its current form] speak of what "we" will become, for example, do they really have in mind a Chinese peasant or an African tribesman—or are such people simply irrelevant to the future? Will the world of computers and information technology generate so much wealth and automation that no one will have to work? And if so, is that really a desirable future? In a classic Jewish story, a pious carter dies and God grants his heartfelt desire to continue to be a carter in the World to Come. The extinctionists are wrong to think that failing bodies are our only problem and better minds our only aspiration—just as they are wrong to ignore the real human hardships that could be ameliorated by a truly human, rather than post-human, progress. At best, they foresee a world that people like *themselves* would like. It is a narrow vision of the human good.

Charles T. Rubin, New Atlantis, *Spring 2003.*

matter of days. Dangerous replicators could easily be too tough, small, and rapidly spreading to stop—at least if we make no preparation. We have trouble enough controlling viruses and fruit flies.

Among the cognoscenti of nanotechnology, this threat has become known as the "gray goo problem." Though masses of uncontrolled replicators need not be gray or gooey, the term "gray goo" emphasizes that replicators able to obliterate life might be less inspiring than a single species of crabgrass. They might be superior in an evolutionary sense, but this need not make them valuable.

The gray goo threat makes one thing perfectly clear: We cannot afford certain kinds of accidents with replicating assemblers.

Gray goo would surely be a depressing ending to our human adventure on Earth, far worse than mere fire or ice, and one that could stem from a simple laboratory accident. Oops.

Uncontrolled Self-Replication

It is most of all the power of destructive self-replication in genetics, nanotechnology, and robotics (GNR) that should give us pause. Self-replication is the modus operandi of genetic engineering, which uses the machinery of the cell to replicate its designs, and the prime danger underlying gray goo in nanotechnology. Stories of run-amok robots like the Borg [a robotic race from *Star Trek: The Next Generation*], replicating or mutating to escape from the ethical constraints imposed on them by their creators, are well established in our science fiction books and movies. It is even possible that self-replication may be more fundamental than we thought, and hence harder—or even impossible—to control. A recent article by Stuart Kauffman in *Nature* titled "Self-Replication: Even Peptides Do It" discusses the discovery that a 32-amino-acid peptide can "autocatalyse its own synthesis." We don't know how widespread this ability is, but Kauffman notes that it may hint at "a route to self-reproducing molecular systems on a basis far wider than Watson-Crick base-pairing [the standard pairing in DNA]."

In truth, we have had in hand for years clear warnings of the dangers inherent in widespread knowledge of GNR technologies—of the possibility of knowledge alone enabling mass destruction. But these warnings haven't been widely publicized; the public discussions have been clearly inadequate. There is no profit in publicizing the dangers.

The nuclear, biological, and chemical (NBC) technologies used in 20th-century weapons of mass destruction were and are largely military, developed in government laboratories. In sharp contrast, the 21st-century GNR technologies have clear commercial uses and are being developed almost exclusively by corporate enterprises. In this age of triumphant commercialism, technology—with science as its handmaiden—is delivering a series of almost magical inventions that are the most phenomenally lucrative ever seen. We are aggressively pursuing the promises of these new technologies within the now-unchallenged system of global capitalism and its manifold financial incentives and competitive pressures.

This is the first moment in the history of our planet when any species, by its own voluntary actions, has become a danger to itself—as well as to vast numbers of others. . . .

The Need to Respect Life

I remember from my childhood that my grandmother was strongly against the overuse of antibiotics. She had worked since before the first World War as a nurse and had a commonsense attitude that taking antibiotics, unless they were absolutely necessary, was bad for you.

It is not that she was an enemy of progress. She saw much progress in an almost 70-year nursing career; my grandfather, a diabetic, benefited greatly from the improved treatments that became available in his lifetime. But she, like many level-headed people, would probably think it greatly arrogant for us, now, to be designing a robotic "replacement species," when we obviously have so much trouble making relatively simple things work, and so much trouble managing—or even understanding—ourselves.

I realize now that she had an awareness of the nature of the order of life, and of the necessity of living with and respecting that order. With this respect comes a necessary humility that we, with our early-21st-century chutzpah [audacity], lack at our peril. The commonsense view, grounded in this respect, is often right, in advance of the scientific evidence. The clear fragility and inefficiencies of the human-made systems we have built should give us all pause; the fragility of the systems I have worked on certainly humbles me.

We should have learned a lesson from the making of the first atomic bomb and the resulting arms race. We didn't do well then, and the parallels to our current situation are troubling. . . .

Now, as then, we are creators of new technologies and stars of the imagined future, driven—this time by great financial rewards and global competition—despite the clear dangers, hardly evaluating what it may be like to try to live in a world that is the realistic outcome of what we are creating and imagining.

Defenses Against the Future

In 1947, *The Bulletin of the Atomic Scientists* began putting a Doomsday Clock on its cover. For more than 50 years, it has shown an estimate of the relative nuclear danger we have faced, reflecting the changing international conditions. The hands on the clock have moved 15 times and today, standing at nine minutes to midnight, reflect continuing and real danger from nuclear weapons. The recent addition of India and Pakistan to the list of nuclear powers has increased the threat of failure of the nonproliferation goal, and this danger was reflected by moving the hands closer to midnight in 1998.

In our time, how much danger do we face, not just from nuclear weapons, but from all of these technologies? How high are the extinction risks?

The philosopher John Leslie has studied this question and concluded that the risk of human extinction is at least 30 percent, while Ray Kurzweil believes we have "a better than even chance of making it through," with the caveat that he has "always been accused of being an optimist." Not only are these estimates not encouraging, but they do not include the probability of many horrid outcomes that lie short of extinction.

Faced with such assessments, some serious people are already suggesting that we simply move beyond Earth as quickly as possible. We would colonize the galaxy using von Neumann probes, which hop from star system to star system, replicating as they go. This step will almost certainly be necessary 5 billion years from now (or sooner if our solar system is disastrously impacted by the impending collision of our galaxy with the Andromeda galaxy within the next 3 billion years), but if we take Kurzweil and Moravec at their word it might be necessary by the middle of this century.

What are the moral implications here? If we must move beyond Earth this quickly in order for the species to survive, who accepts the responsibility for the fate of those (most of us, after all) who are left behind? And even if we scatter to the stars, isn't it likely that we may take our problems with us or find, later, that they have followed us? The fate of our species on Earth and our fate in the galaxy seem inextricably linked.

Another idea is to erect a series of shields to defend against each of the dangerous technologies. The Strategic Defense Initiative, proposed by the [Ronald] Reagan administration, was an attempt to design such a shield against the threat of a nuclear attack from the Soviet Union. But as [science fiction author and inventor] Arthur C. Clarke, who was privy to discussions about the project, observed: "Though it might be possible, at vast expense, to construct local defense systems that would 'only' let through a few percent of ballistic missiles, the much touted idea of a national umbrella was nonsense. Luis Alvarez, perhaps the greatest experimental physicist of this century, remarked to me that the advocates of such schemes were 'very bright guys with no common sense.'"

Clarke continued: "Looking into my often cloudy crystal ball, I suspect that a total defense might indeed be possible in a century or so. But the technology involved would produce, as a by-product, weapons so terrible that no one would bother with anything as primitive as ballistic missiles."

In *Engines of Creation*, Eric Drexler proposed that we build an active nanotechnological shield—a form of immune system for the biosphere—to defend against dangerous replicators of all kinds that might escape from laboratories or otherwise be maliciously created. But the shield he proposed would itself be extremely dangerous—nothing could prevent it from developing autoimmune problems and attacking the biosphere itself.

Similar difficulties apply to the construction of shields against robotics and genetic engineering. These technologies are too powerful to be shielded against in the time frame of interest; even if it were possible to implement defensive shields, the side effects of their development would be at least as dangerous as the technologies we are trying to protect against.

Limit Technology to Avoid Extinction

These possibilities are all thus either undesirable or unachievable or both. The only realistic alternative I see is relinquishment: to limit development of the technologies that are too dangerous, by limiting our pursuit of certain kinds of knowledge.

Yes, I know, knowledge is good, as is the search for new truths. We have been seeking knowledge since ancient times. Aristotle opened his *Metaphysics* with the simple statement: "All men by nature desire to know." We have, as a bedrock value in our society, long agreed on the value of open access to information, and recognize the problems that arise with attempts to restrict access to and development of knowledge. In recent times, we have come to revere scientific knowledge.

But despite the strong historical precedents, if open access to and unlimited development of knowledge henceforth puts us all in clear danger of extinction, then common sense demands that we reexamine even these basic, long-held beliefs. . . .

The new Pandora's boxes of genetics, nanotechnology, and robotics are almost open, yet we seem hardly to have noticed.

Ideas can't be put back in a box; unlike uranium or pluto-nium, they don't need to be mined and refined, and they can be freely copied. Once they are out, they are out. [British statesman Winston] Churchill remarked, in a famous left-handed compliment, that the American people and their lead-ers "invariably do the right thing, after they have examined every other alternative." In this case, however, we must act more presciently, as to do the right thing only at last may be to lose the chance to do it at all.

As [Henry David] Thoreau said, "We do not ride on the railroad; it rides upon us"; and this is what we must fight, in our time. The question is, indeed, Which is to be master? Will we survive our technologies? . . .

Knowing is not a rationale for not acting. Can we doubt that knowledge has become a weapon we wield against our-selves?

The experiences of the atomic scientists clearly show the need to take personal responsibility, the danger that things will move too fast, and the way in which a process can take on a life of its own. We can, as they did, create insurmount-able problems in almost no time flat. We must do more think-ing up front if we are not to be similarly surprised and shocked by the consequences of our inventions.

My continuing professional work is on improving the reli-ability of software. Software is a tool, and as a toolbuilder I must struggle with the uses to which the tools I make are put. I have always believed that making software more reliable, given its many uses, will make the world a safer and better place; if I were to come to believe the opposite, then I would be morally obligated to stop this work. I can now imagine such a day may come.

This all leaves me not angry but at least a bit melancholic. Henceforth, for me, progress will be somewhat bittersweet.

Do you remember the beautiful penultimate scene in [the film] *Manhattan* where Woody Allen is lying on his couch and talking into a tape recorder? He is writing a short story about people who are creating unnecessary, neurotic problems for themselves, because it keeps them from dealing with more unsolvable, terrifying problems about the universe.

He leads himself to the question, "Why is life worth living?" and to consider what makes it worthwhile for him: Groucho Marx, Willie Mays, the second movement of the *Jupiter Symphony*, Louis Armstrong's recording of "Potato Head Blues," Swedish movies, Flaubert's *Sentimental Education*, Marlon Brando, Frank Sinatra, the apples and pears by Cézanne, the crabs at Sam Wo's, and, finally, the showstopper: his love Tracy's face.

Each of us has our precious things, and as we care for them we locate the essence of our humanity. In the end, it is because of our great capacity for caring that I remain optimistic we will confront the dangerous issues now before us.

Periodical Bibliography

The following articles have been selected to supplement the diverse views presented in this chapter.

Stephen Bertman "With Knowledge Comes Responsibility: Technology and Human Values in a Warp-Speed World," *Vital Speeches of the Day*, March 15, 2005.

Andy Borowitz "Danger, Stupid Human! Danger!" *CIO*, Fall/Winter 2003.

Andy Crouch "When Backward Is Forward: Christmas May Be the Best Argument against Genetic Enhancement," *Christianity Today*, December 2004.

Marcy Darnovsky "Embryo Cloning and Beyond," *Tikkun*, July/August 2002.

Henry T. Greely "Man and Superman: If We Choose to Enhance Our Bodies and Minds It Won't Be Without Risk, but That's No Reason to Pull Up the Drawbridge," *New Scientist*, August 5, 2006.

Raymond Kurzweil "Promise and Peril of the 21st Century," *CIO*, Fall/Winter 2003.

Jerry Large "Evolution Leaps Past Darwin as We Become One with Machines," *Seattle Times*, July 31, 2006.

Stephen Leahy "Biotech Hope and Hype: The Genetics Revolution Has Failed to Deliver, Says Stephen Leahy," *Maclean's*, September 30, 2002.

James M. Pethokoukis, Simon Smith, and Eric Cohen "Humanity 2.0," *U.S. News & World Report Online*, August 29, 2003. www.usnews.com.

Michael Stroh "Future Jocks: In the Next Decade, Cutting-Edge Gene Research May Cure Hundreds of Diseases. It May Also Help Cheating Athletes Build Superhuman Strength," *Science World*, September 27, 2002.

For Further Discussion

Chapter 1

1. According to physicist Jonathan Huebner (as cited in David Cox's viewpoint), technological innovation peaked in 1873 and has been on the decline since then. Building on Huebner's claim, Cox asserts that most inventions of the most recent centuries have been novelties meant to amuse people rather than significant, revolutionary discoveries. After cataloging the technology you or your friends possess or utilize on a daily basis, decide whether Cox's argument appears true. Now looking beyond your personal gear, consider whether Cox's claim is an accurate assessment of inventiveness over the past fifty years. Is Cox's opinion of technological innovation correct, or does it seem too pessimistic? Explain your answer.

2. Comparing the arguments given by Brent Staples and those offered by Jeffrey Boase and his colleagues, decide whether you think the Internet is a benefit or detriment to social interaction. In framing your answer, include your own experiences with the Internet: In what ways have you found the Internet isolating? In what ways have you found it liberating?

3. Doug Saunders claims that current civilization has no need for robotic machines because there are enough people who are willing to do the most menial tasks for wages. Marshall Brain, on the other hand, states that robots are already taking jobs away from people. Which argument do you find more convincing, or is it possible that both authors are correct? Explain.

Chapter 2

1. Clifford Stoll contends that modern classrooms rely too much on computer learning. He states that this has resulted in students who lack basic problem solving skills and who know how to download material but not understand it. Mortimer Zuckerman, however, insists that computers belong in the classroom because students need to master computers to participate in a computer-driven future. After examining both arguments, give your opinion about computers in education. Do you think they encourage students to take the easy way out of problem solving? Or are computers vital to a learning environment that has to change with the times? Is there a way to satisfy both Stoll and Zuckerman? Explain your answer.

2. Ejovi Nuwere argues that the term "digital divide" masks the real social problem of racial and class division in America. He asserts that simply providing more computers to underprivileged children will not close the "divide." Do you think Nuwere is correct? If so, what do you think can be done to solve the "digital divide" crisis? If you believe Nuwere is incorrect, how do you respond to his arguments?

3. After considering the opinions of Susan Smith Nash and David Sobel, describe how you feel about the current tech-savvy generation. Are children today smarter and more sophisticated with technology than past generations? Are there costs to being so tech-savvy? What are the benefits and problems children experience in being brought up in the computer age?

Chapter 3

1. Do some research on the topic of nanotechnology. What are the promises of this science and what are the possible risks? Do you believe, as Sonia Arrison does, that scientists should regulate this field so that excessive rules will

not stifle innovation? Or do you side with J. Clarence Davies in claiming that government oversight is needed because most people are not even aware that nanotechnology—and its unknown dangers—are already bound up in many commonly used products?

2. Michael Gazzaniga believes that therapeutic cloning should not be banned by the government because it holds the promise of curing disease and helping severely afflicted individuals. Leon R. Kass argues that therapeutic cloning is an unproven medical technique that, if sanctioned, would likely lead to human cloning. Which viewpoint do you find more persuasive? Why? In your answer, be sure to address Kass's fear that therapeutic cloning would open the door to human cloning.

Chapter 4

1. David Merriman's proposal to allow genetic enhancement of future generations is based on the notion that such manipulation is ethical and possibly beneficial. Other commentators have even suggested that parents would have an obligation to enhance their children, for to not do so would handicap them in a world dominated by enhanced peers. Conversely, Bill McKibbon contends that each enhancement would never be "good enough" because newer, better enhancements would always be perfected, rendering past enhancements obsolete. What do you think about genetic enhancements? Should every person have the right to be "better" than he or she is, or should enhancements be banned so that McKibbon's "arms race" analogy would never occur? Explain your answer.

2. Ray Kurzweil's view of a future world in which technology and humanity have merged is very optimistic and seductive. He insists that as fanciful as his vision seems, it is likely that current technology trends would have looked just as far-fetched to people of past centuries. Do you

think that Kurzweil's prediction of humanity and machinery reaching a Singularity is inevitable? Why? Are there any elements of his vision that you think are just impossible? Why do you think so? Then, consider Bill Joy's critique of Kurzweil's prophecy. Do you think his fear that realizing Kurzweil's dream may lead to a dystopian future is any more sound than Kurzweil's rosy vision? Explain.

Organizations to Contact

The editors have compiled the following list of organizations concerned with the issues debated in this book. The descriptions are derived from materials provided by the organizations. All have publications or information available for interested readers. The list was compiled on the date of publication of the present volume; the information provided here may change. Be aware that many organizations take several weeks or longer to respond to inquiries, so allow as much time as possible.

Biotechnology Industry Organization (BIO)
1225 Eye St. NW, Suite 400, Washington, DC 20005
(202) 962-9200
e-mail: info@bio.org
Web site: www.bio.org

BIO is an organization composed of companies working in the biotechnology industry. BIO serves as lobbying group for the industry, advocating for its member companies and promoting legislation that is beneficial to the advancement of the industry. The organization also seeks to provide accurate information about biotechnology to the public through publications such as *BIO Bulletin, BIO News,* and the book *Biotech for All.*

Center for Bioethics and Human Dignity (CBHD)
2065 Half Day Rd., Bannockburn, IL 60015
(847) 317-8180 • fax: (847) 317-8101
e-mail: info@cbhd.org
Web site: www.cbhd.org

CBHD investigates the ethical issues of emerging biotechnology from a Christian perspective. It publishes position statements and overviews on many issues including cloning, euthanasia, and stem cell research. The center also sponsors several conferences each year concerning bioethics.

Center for Democracy and Technology (CDT)
1634 Eye St. NW, #1100, Washington, DC   20006
(202) 637-9800 • fax: (202) 637-0968
Web site: www.cdt.org

CDT seeks to promote open and democratic public policy with regards to Internet use in the era of modern globalization. The main issues the organization advocates for are freedom of expression and access for all on the Internet, as well as privacy and protection from surveillance for those who use the Internet. Policy briefs, reports, and articles relating to Internet access and control are available on the group's Web site.

Computing Research Association (CRA)
1100 Seventeenth St. NW, Suite 507, Washington, DC   20036
(202) 234-2111 • fax: (202) 667-1066
Web site: www.cra.org

CRA represents organizations that participate in all areas of computer research. Member organizations include educational institutions, professional societies, and private and government industries. The association seeks to promote an increased knowledge of the computer research field and to advocate for a government policy that benefits not only the industry but the whole of society. Publications by CRA include *Computing Research News* and *CRA Bulletin*.

Council for Responsible Genetics (CRG)
5 Upland Rd., Suite 3, Cambridge, MA   02140
(617) 868-0870 • fax: (617) 491-5344
e-mail: crg@gene-watch.org
Web site: www.gene-watch.org

CRG is an organization dedicated to involving and educating the public in the ongoing debate concerning genetic technology. CRG monitors and reports on issues related to genetic experimentation, cloning, and biopharming. Its bimonthly publication *Gene Watch* reports on the social, ethical, and environmental issues associated with these and other emerging biotechnologies.

Electronic Frontier Foundation (EFF)
454 Shotwell St., San Francisco, CA 94110
(415) 436-9333 • fax: (415) 436-9993
e-mail: information@eff.org
Web site: www.eff.org

EFF works to protect consumer rights, freedom of expression, and privacy in relation to digital technologies, primarily the Internet. Through educational programs, government policy advising, and lawsuits, the EFF attempts to influence and shape digital culture in the United States. General information and descriptions of court cases relating to topics such as privacy, fair use, file sharing, and free speech are available on the organization's Web site.

Electronic Privacy Information Center (EPIC)
1718 Connecticut Ave. NW, Suite 200
Washington, DC 20009
(202) 483-1140 • fax: (202) 483-1248
Web site: www.epic.org

EPIC is a public interest organization that provides information on constitutional issues, such as freedom of speech and the right to privacy, as they relate to society in the ever-changing electronic information age. The publication *EPIC Alert*, an online newsletter, can be accessed on the organization's Web site. Additionally, EPIC publishes numerous reports and books concerning civil liberties.

Institute on Biotechnology and the Human Future
565 W. Adams St., Chicago, IL 60661
(312) 906-5337
e-mail: info@thehumanfuture.org
Web site: www.thehumanfuture.org

The Institute on Biotechnology and the Human Future assesses the impact of technology on society from a cultural and ethical perspective with the goal of promoting those ideals that best promote human life and progress. Topics of inquiry include nanotechnology, genetic technology, and human cloning. Commentaries on these and other topics can be found on the organization's Web site.

Institute for Ethics and Emerging Technologies (IEET)
Williams 229B, Trinity College, Hartford, CT   06106
(860) 297-2376
e-mail: director@ieet.org
Web site: www.ieet.org

The IEET is an organization seeking to publicize the debate on the ethical use of emerging technologies. Scholars from around the world contribute to the conversation on the use of technologies such as invitro fertilization, stem cell research, and life extension. The IEET provides a forum for individuals to debate the proliferation of technology without taking sides that polarize the issues. The organization's Web site provides many essays and reports concerning the use of technology in society.

Institute for Global Communication (IGC)
PO Box 29047, San Francisco, CA   94129-0047
e-mail: support@igc.apc.org
Web site: www.igc.org

The IGC was formed in 1987 to provide Web-hosting for grassroots organizations with human rights and environmental agendas. These networks offered organizations worldwide the opportunity to speak to a wide audience about their concerns and issues. Networks still hosted by IGC include PeaceNet, EcoNet, WomensNet, and AntiRacismNet.

International Society for Technology in Education (ISTE)
1710 Rhode Island Ave. NW, Suite 900
Washington, DC   20036
(866) 654-4777 • fax: (202) 861-0888
e-mail: iste@iste.org
Web site: www.iste.org

ISTE works to advance the use of technology in education through development, research, leadership, and advocacy. Internationally, the organization presents a forum for the exchange of information concerning improved methods of technology use in education. Publications by ISTE include *Learning and Leading with Technology*, the *Journal of Research on Technology in Education*, and numerous books providing new approaches to incorporating technology into educational programs.

National School Boards Association (NSBA)
1680 Duke St., Alexandria, VA   22314
(703) 838-6722 • fax: (703) 683-7590
e-mail: info@nsba.org
Web site: www.nsba.org

The NSBA established the Institute for the Transfer of Technology to Education (ITTE) in order to promote technology as an essential tool in education. The organization emphasizes the importance of technological literacy in the modern world. The NSBA publishes *American School Board Journal* and *School Board News*, both of which contain articles discussing the importance of technology in education.

U.S. Department of Education
400 Maryland Ave. SW, Washington, DC   20202
(800) 872-5327
Web site: www.ed.gov

The U.S. Department of Education works to ensure that all students in the United States are offered an equal opportunity to receive an education. Incorporation of technology into the American education system is one of the many concerns of this governmental department. The Office of Educational Technology (OET) works to implement educational technology policies, and provides teacher's guides for employing technology in an educational setting. In 2005 the OET published the *National Education Technology Plan*, which outlines the relationship between technology and education in the United States.

U.S. Department of Energy, Office of Science

1000 Independence Ave. SW, Washington, DC   20585
(800) 342-5363 • fax: (202) 586-4403
Web site: www.science.doe.gov

The U.S. Department of Energy's Office of Science is responsible for many of the technology-related projects undertaken by the U.S. government. Energy-related technologies such as fusion and nuclear are one concern of the Office of Science; the Human Genome Project and other related biotechnology projects are overseen by this department as well. The Department of Energy Web site provides links to all the areas of the Office of Science and offers in-depth fact sheets on each of the projects it has undertaken.

World Future Society

7910 Woodmont Ave., Suite 450, Bethesda, MD   20814
(301) 656-8274
e-mail: info@wfs.org
Web site: www.wfs.org

The World Future Society is an organization dedicated to examining the impact of social and technological developments on the future. The society and its publications provide individuals with an opportunity to debate about coming events and offer ideas about how to make changes that will alter the future. The *Futurist* is the bimonthly magazine of the World Future Society; other publications include *Futures Research Quarterly, Future Survey, Future Times,* and *Futurist Update.*

Bibliography of Books

Ronald Bailey   *Liberation Biology: The Scientific and Moral Case for the Biotech Revolution.* Amherst, NY: Prometheus, 2005.

Maria Bakardjieva *Internet Society: The Internet in Everyday Life.* Thousand Oaks, CA: Sage, 2005.

David M. Berube   *Nano-Hype: The Truth Behind the Nanotechnology Buzz.* Amherst, NY: Prometheus, 2005.

Amy Sue Bix   *Inventing Ourselves Out of Jobs? America's Debate over Technological Unemployment, 1929–1981.* Baltimore: Johns Hopkins University Press, 2001.

John Seely Brown *The Social Life of Information.* Boston: Harvard Business School Press, 2002.
and Paul Duguid

Benjamin M.   *The Digital Divide: Facing a Crisis or Creating a Myth?* Cambridge, MA: MIT Press, 2001.
Compaine, ed.

Larry Cuban   *Oversold and Underused: Computers in the Classroom.* Cambridge, MA: Harvard University Press, 2003.

Jan A. G. M. van *The Deepening Divide: Inequality in the Information Society.* Thousand Oaks, CA: Sage, 2005.
Dijk

Editors of   *Understanding Nanotechnology.* New York: Warner, 2002.
Scientific
American

Francis Fukuyama   *Our Posthuman Future: Consequences of the Biotechnology Revolution.* New York: Farrar, Straus & Giroux, 2002.

Joel Garreau   *Radical Evolution: The Promise and Peril of Enhancing Our Minds, Our Bodies—and What It Means to Be Human.* New York: Doubleday, 2005.

Andrea R. Gooden   *Computers in the Classroom: How Teachers and Students Are Using Technology to Transform Learning.* San Francisco: Jossey-Bass, 1996.

Philip E. N. Howard and Steve Jones, eds.   *Society Online: The Internet in Context.* Thousand Oaks, CA: Sage, 2004.

James Hughes   *Citizen Cyborg: Why Democratic Societies Must Respond to the Redesigned Human of the Future.* Cambridge, MA: Westview, 2004.

Institute of Medicine   *Stem Cells and the Future of Regenerative Medicine.* Washington, DC: National Academy Press, 2002.

Leon R. Kass   *Life, Liberty, and the Defense of Dignity: The Challenge for Bioethics.* Washington, DC: AEI Press, 2004.

Ray Kurzweil   *The Age of Spiritual Machines: When Computers Exceed Human Intelligence.* New York: Penguin, 2000.

Ray Kurzweil   *The Singularity Is Near: When Humans Transcend Biology.* New York: Viking, 2005.

Jane Maienschein   *Whose View of Life? Embryos, Cloning, and Stem Cells*. Cambridge, MA: Harvard University Press, 2003.

Maxwell J. Mehlman   *Wondergenes: Genetic Enhancement and the Future of Society*. Bloomington: Indiana University Press, 2003.

Alondra Nelson, Thuy Linh N. Tu, and Hines Alicia Headlam, eds.   *TechniColor: Race, Technology, and Everyday Life*. New York: New York University Press, 2001.

Robert D. Oberst   *2020 Web Vision: How the Internet Will Revolutionize Future Homes, Business and Society*. Parkland, FL: Universal, 2001.

Todd Oppenheimer   *The Flickering Mind: Saving Education from the False Promise of Technology*. New York: Random House, 2004.

Ann B. Parsons   *Proteus Effect: Stem Cells and Their Promise for Medicine*. Washington, DC: Joseph Henry, 2006.

President's Council on Bioethics   *Human Cloning and Human Dignity: The Report of the President's Council on Bioethics*. New York: Public Affairs, 2002.

Mark A. Ratner and Daniel Ratner   *Nanotechnology: A Gentle Introduction to the Next Big Idea*. Upper Saddle River, NJ: Prentice Hall, 2002.

Toby Shelley   *Nanotechnology: New Promises, New Dangers*. New York: Zed, 2006.

Lee M. Silver   *Remaking Eden: How Genetic Engineering and Cloning Will Transform the American Family*. New York: HarperPerennial, 1998.

Mark Warschauer   *Technology and Social Inclusion: Rethinking the Digital Divide*. Cambridge, MA: MIT Press, 2004.

Brent Waters and Ronald Cole-Turner, eds.   *God and the Embryo: Religious Voices on Stem Cells and Cloning*. Washington, DC: Georgetown University Press, 2003.

Simon Young   *Designer Evolution: A Transhumanist Manifesto*. Amherst, NY: Prometheus, 2005.

Index

A

Advanced Cell Technology (technology firm), 159

Advertising Age (magazine), 16

The Age of Spiritual Machines (Kurzweil), 186

Aging, nanotechnology and, 170, 175

Air travel, diseases and, 38

Allen, Woody, 196–197

Altruism, gene therapy and, 150–151

Alvarez, Luis, 194

Amazon, 110, 112

Amazon.com, 110

Amish groups, resisting technology, 37

Andromeda Galaxy, 194

AOL, 118

Aristotle, 195

Arnhart, Larry, 146

Arnold, Marcus, 52

Artificial intelligence (AI)
definition of human and, 178
machines and, 58
nanobots and, 173–175
predicted to exceed human intelligence, 176–177
as robotic revolution, 169, 175–177
telepathic communication and, 173–174
weapons and, 175

ASIMO robot, 58

Asimov, Isaac, 62

Assemblers, molecular-level, 188, 189, 191

Atari Sunnyvale Research Lab, 30

Automated self-service systems, 56–58

Automated systems. *See* Robots

Automobiles, navigational systems for, 29

B

"Baby Einstein" video series, 160

Ban, on cloning, 134

Barnes & Noble, 110

Benefits of technology. *See* Society, benefiting from technology

BIO (Biotechnology Industry Organization), 203

Bioethics Council, 139–140

Biological arms race, 161–163

Biological enhancements. *See* Enhancement of children, opposition to; Enhancement of Children, toleration of; Germline genetic engineering

Biomedical cloning, 139, 140

Biotechnology Industry Organization (BIO), 203

Biotechnology. *See* Genetic biotechnology

BJ's (warehouse club) self-service, 56

Black, Ira, 142

Boase, Jeffrey, 40, 44

Boomer generation, 94, 97

Borg (robotic race), 191

Bostrom, Nick, 151

Brain-to-brain communication. *See* Artificial Intelligence

Brave New World (Huxley), 149